Increase Profit From Your Women's Clothing Store

THE SMALL BUSINESS SUCCESS GUIDE

ISBN: 1508814007
ISBN-13: 978-1508814009

DEDICATION

To small business owners everywhere.

CONTENTS

Why do you need this book?   1

1   The profit in sales techniques   4

2   Look like a million dollars   10

3   Chewing up the profits   20

4   Paper money   25

5   More sales, less budget   41

6   Small cost, big impact   55

7   Make money answering the telephone   63

8   Time is money   66

9   Social money   72

10 Right on the money   76

The buck stops here   81

WHY DO YOU NEED THIS BOOK?

Do you want to increase the profit you make from your women's retail clothing shop?

Do you want some easy to follow tips for business success? Yes? Well you have come to the right place.

In this book you will find easy tips and tricks to improve your sales and profitability. And it all starts with your marketing.

Marketing covers everything aspect of your business, not just your advertising. It covers the quality of your product and the way you answer the phone. Your marketing will make you stand out from your competition. It will produce customer loyalty by providing a great experience as well as delivering a great product.

With just a few small and easy changes, a few minutes of a day you can turn your clothing store into a small business success story.

The three principles of a successful clothing store are.

- Cultivate
- Grow
- Thrive

CULTIVATE

The first three chapters of this book will help you cultivate your existing business. You will find tips and tricks to increase your sales (and your profit) from your existing customers. There is no point adding new customers if you cannot look after the ones you already have.

GROW

Chapters four to nine discuss advertising and promotion methods to grow your customer base and improve customer loyalty. You will learn about guerrilla marketing techniques and how to apply them to your boutique. Social media, television, radio and the more traditional flyers and newsletters are all covered in detail. There are ideas for all budgets, but mostly for small budgets.

THRIVE

The last chapter deals with managing your business for long term success.

What are you waiting for? Start growing your business now!

CULTIVATE

Create an environment to sell as much as possible to customers already coming to your store.

1 THE PROFIT IN SALES TECHNIQUES
Sell more to your existing customers

Did you know it costs less to sell to your existing customers then it does to gain new customers? In fact it costs five to seven times more to gain new customers than it does to retain them.

How do you sell more to your existing customers? Improve your sales techniques. Without gaining any new customers or incurring any marketing expenses, you can make more money.

You can follow all the strategies outlined later in this book and increase the amount of people coming to your store. But if you cannot sell them anything, all your time, effort and money has been wasted.

Sales techniques are a combination of different processes and skills that successful sales people use.

In this chapter you will find the following sales techniques:

- Understand how a buyer makes the decision to buy
- Catch the sales that slip through
- How to help the customer, rather than sell to the customer.

Start improving your selling techniques now!

#1 WELCOME

Greet your customer warmly on entering your store. Many shoppers complain they are never greeted on entering a store.

Ensure you and your staff:

- greet regular customers by name;
- welcome strangers;
- attend customers promptly; and
- wear a smile.

#2 EYE CONTACT

Making eye contact with a customer displays a sincere interest to help. A significant 72% of shoppers complain that sales assistants do not make eye contact when speaking to a customer, and appear to be bothered when the customer asks a question.

If you cannot serve the customer immediately, make eye contact with the customer and smile in acknowledgement.

#3 KNOW YOUR PRODUCT

You need to know what you sell. You need to be able to communicate what you sell to your customer. If you do not know what you sell, how can you tell the customer who walks in the front door?

You should ensure all staff are aware of what your store currently stocks. You should also let them know about stock that is on order. They can tell the customer with the hope the customer will come back when the stock has arrived.

What do you sell in your store? Swimwear? Evening wear? Make sure your staff know.

#4 HELP PEOPLE BUY

Salesmen: love them or loathe them, they are a necessity. Without salespeople, businesses do not exist and established businesses can fail.

But not everyone is a natural at sales, some need extra help. Take a look at the following example.

Have you ever walked into a store to browse, only to have the assistant comment on every single garment that you pull off the rack? Sure, the assistant is doing their job. But is it effective? What do you, as buyer, feel towards this person who watches your every move and tries to sell you everything you look at: warmth or irritation? Does this happen in your store?

Sales are not a matter of the seller telling the person to buy. There is information that must be exchanged. The exchange of information is called communication. And, as every successful salesperson will tell you, communication is what sales is all about.

Patrick Forsyth, of Marketing on a Tight Budget, [1] has identified seven stages that the buyer's mind goes through on the way to making a purchase:

- I am important and I want to be respected.
- Consider my needs.
- How will your ideas help me?
- What are the facts?
- What are the snags?
- What shall I do about them?

- I approve.

For the sale to be effective, salesperson needs to be familiar with each of these stages in decision making, and be able to respond to each stage satisfactorily. If there is a breakdown somewhere along this path, chances are the buyer will not feel confident, will hesitate, and will walk away, without the purchase.

Note that these steps and their responses involve a two way flow of communication between the buyer and the seller. It is NOT one sided.

#5 LET THE CUSTOMER LOOK

Let the customer look around. Let her touch a garment without having to suffer a dissertation on the quality, cut, style, color, fashion, etc.

#6 ARE YOU LISTENING

Telling is not selling. Selling is listening.

When your customer asks you a question or speaks generally, listen. You can actively listen your way to success by asking good question. Listen and attempt to understand the answers and the questions you get from your customers.

#7 APPROACH ME

Be approachable and quietly chatty, without overpowering your customers. Remember the above stages, use them in sequence and in step with the buyer, and sell the benefits.

Using this technique should see more sales being made, more repeat business, and more profit.

#8 IT IS NOT WHAT YOU SAY BUT HOW YOU SAY IT

Research has shown that clients are more likely to be positively influenced by the salesperson whose speech patterns are similar to their own.[2]

When speaking with your next client, modify your own speech patterns to fit with theirs. For example, you are talking with your client and you notice that their natural speech pattern is slower and the volume is softer than yours. You should respond by slowing down your speech and softening your volume to match. By doing so you will find that your words are more thoroughly understood and your message or advice is clearer, resulting in a greater likelihood that you will get the initial sale and retain this client's repeat business.

When you first greet your client, remember to listen out for their speech patterns and try to fit in with them.

#9 CATCHING THE SALES THAT SLIP THROUGH

Do you find sales seem to slip through your fingers? Let us have a look at what could be going wrong.

The optimum way of selling is to adhere to the following sequence.

1. The retailer needs to recognize and cater to the customer's need to feel important and respected.
2. Next, the retailer should cater to the customer's specific need and provide ideas that will help them.
3. Give them the facts, the snags, advice and your approval of the purchase.

Missing out one of those stages will affect whether or not a sale goes through. Sometimes the seller progresses through the stages out of step with the buyer. The seller must not work through the sequence too quickly or too slowly for the buyer.

#10 SELL BENEFITS, NOT THE PRODUCT

Did you sell the product, the clothes, rather than the benefits to the buyer? It is not enough to buy a green dress. The green dress needs to be useful.

- Does it bring out the color of your customer's eyes?
- Is the dress so versatile that it can be worn anywhere, dressed up or dressed down.

It may be the kind of dress that could be worn to a christening, a garden party, a race day, a restaurant, a 21st birthday, an anniversary, an awards night, a concert.

On this occasion perhaps the buyer had no immediate need for the dress, but the benefits of the dress spelt out to the customer won the sale.

Get excited about your product. The features and benefits may be old to you, but they are new to the customer. Keep your energy up and present with passion.

It is your responsibility to ensure that the client understands your services and the standards of quality that may reasonably be expected.

#11 DO NOT SELL, HELP

Most people can spot a salesperson a mile away. And once they have spotted one, what do they do? Walk the other way, look down, and put up the old "Do not try to sell me anything" wall. So how do you sell your stock to these people? Shift the focus. Do not sell, help.

Most customers want to enjoy a friendly relationship with store owners. In an era of automated, online everything, customers need to feel that they count. They will be attracted to the human element. After product, customers want service.

What customer service means to the customer (not the salesperson) is someone who is interested in them as an individual. So chat to the customer

7

without being nosey.

A way of doing this is to move the focus away from selling and on to your own experiences. Talk about what has been happening in your own life first, then gradually move to the customer's life. Once a rapport has been established, they will open up. When the lines of communication are open, you will be able to change the focus back to the clothes, with a much greater chance of making a sale.

Once a customer has decided to buy some clothing you will be able to value-add the service. This is when you can suggest accessories such as a belt or a necklace.

#12 GETTING TO KNOW YOU

Take advantage of the opportunity to get to know your customers individually. Try to get to know what your customers want and need out of your business, then tailor your products and service to suit.

#13 EGO - IT IS NOT A DIRTY WORD

No-one's ego can be fed enough. Always compliment your customer's appearance. Act as though you are interested in what they tell you about their lives. Be tactful in the way you do this. Try not to come across as superficial.

#14 NO WASTED TIME

There is no need to think you have wasted your time listening to clients who do not buy after you tell them the price. You still did your job as a business owner. You consulted, assisted and provided service.

When money is less of an issue, these clients will return to your store, because of your great service and personal assistance.

#15 THANK YOU

Do whatever it takes to keep your customers **your** customers. The easiest and most effective way to do this is to follow up after a sale with a thank you note or email. Include advertisements for future in-store promotions. More about promotions later in this book.

#16 POSITIVES ATTRACT

Personalities are contagious. If your attitude is positive, your customers' will be too. Positive attitudes make sales.

#17 REASON TO CHARGE

Pricing is an ongoing issue for all businesses. How to price? When to reduce and when to increase?

Price is a major player in the battle to wrest market share from your competitors. How the product is priced creates an image for the product. It represents its value for money and its quality. Ultimately the price greatly affects the consumer's decision-making process, determining to a great extent whether or not they'll buy the product. And retail clothing is no exception.

So how do you price? Think about product differentiation: where your product is so different that you can price accordingly. The more unique your product, the greater flexibility you have in pricing. Do you offer the best service in your town, a point that adds value to your product and allows you to differentiate on price? If this is you, then focus of all of your marketing communications on this point.

Think about cost competitiveness - where you beat the competition because of a low price. Although price wars are not recommended, it is important to stay abreast of the competition and price competitively. The cost of the garments and your profit margins need to be considered carefully.

As a small business owner there is no need to focus wholly on one pricing strategy. Think about how each of these strategies affect you, and how you can use them in your current position. Which strategy you focus on, or how you combine the two, will obviously depend on the positioning of your business in the marketplace.

Look at the direct competition in your area. How many competitors are there? How similar is their clothing style to yours? What is the quality of your garments compared to theirs?

What's the state of the economy in your local trading area? Is your community experiencing hard times or good times? The easiest way to find this out is to look at the state of the local area's main industry. This is a good indication as to how price-sensitive the community is.

Price is a sensitive issue for both business owner and consumer. While you must consider covering your costs, your initial price strategy will set a precedent for pricing in the future. It is more difficult to raise a price than to lower it.

So take a closer look at what is going on competitively and economically around you. This type of investigation will give you a competitive edge. If you are releasing a new fashion label and there is no competition, you will have more leeway with pricing.

CHAPTER SUMMARY

This chapter covered of basic sales techniques including:

- Help people buy
- Catching the sales that slip through
- How to help the customer, rather than sell to the customer.

End of chapter one (1)

2 LOOK LIKE A MILLION BUCKS
Tips for a good looking store

You have improved your sales techniques and have seen an increase in sales from your existing customers. You know if you get the customers in the door, you stand a good chance of making a sale. So the next logical step would be to spend money on some advertising and promotions.

Not yet!

Before you spend any money on advertising or promotions, ask yourself: could the look and feel of your store be putting customers off?

If the customer does not walk through the front door, how can you use your selling techniques?

You can follow all the strategies outlined later in this book and increase the amount of people coming to your store. But if they get to the front door and do not like what they see, they will not come into your store. And if they do not come in, you have wasted your time, effort and money on advertising and promotions.

In this chapter you will find hints, tips and tricks on how to create a good looking store that will encourage your customer to buy! You will learn:

How to look the part from the outside

- What makes a good looking sign
- Your window of opportunity
- How to look the part from the inside

Time to get better looking!

#18 BECOME A SUPER SLEUTH

A major part of being in business involves keeping an eye on your competitor. Become a detective and check out your competition on their home turf. Look at how you can make your business image better than theirs.

Put on that spy hat and scope out the competition with the aid of the following checklist.

Do a drive past and note:

- Are the premises easy to spot from the car as you pass?
- Are they clean and well maintained?
- Is the sign easy to read? Does it clearly state that the business is a clothing store?
- Are business hours posted?
- Is the door open? Or, with air-conditioned stores, does the store look open?
- Does the business look successful?
- Would you be inclined to go in?
- What is the neighborhood like? Is it busy and prosperous, neat or run-down?
- Does the shop seem to suit the area?
- Is public transport available and convenient?
- What are the people on the street wearing?
- What types of cars are in the neighborhood?
- Is parking available and are the parking lots full?
- What strikes you immediately? Write a few notes and describe your first impression of the business. What strikes you immediately (think visuals, smells and sounds)?

After you have driven past, go in and make notes on the following:

- What is your immediate reaction on entering the store?
- How would you describe the atmosphere? Is there music playing, or is it clinically quiet?
- Is the music appropriate?
- Is the room neat and clean or cluttered, spacious or cramped?
- Is the attendant occupied and busy?
- Is a professional and caring image presented to the waiting customers?
- Do the staff wear uniforms and/or present an appropriate impression of the store?
- Are they knowledgeable and helpful?

Apply what you have learnt about your competitors to your shop twice as well!

#19 PERCEPTION IS EVERYTHING

In business you are what you are perceived to be, whether you like it or not. Stand out the front of your store and write down all the negative impressions you pick up. Then ask a honest friend to do it. Compare your notes and decide what needs to be changed.

#20 SUPER DUPER SLEUTHING

Attending trade shows can prove very beneficial to your business. In addition to viewing products, you can gather information, scope out your competitors, and establish and improve communication with manufacturing companies.

#21 STAFF SLEUTHING

Provide your staff with opportunities to attend trade shows and seminars. It is a great way to stimulate employee productivity, increase the amount of expertise, and decrease voluntary turnover.

#22 STAY TIDY

Aim to maintain a pleasant shopping atmosphere. Shabby change rooms, general clutter and untidy sales desks can unfavorably influence a customer's decision to return.

#23 WHAT WAS YOUR NAME AGAIN?

Is the name of your business letting you down?

- A catchy name is an important marketing tool.
- It needs to be easy to remember and easy to say.
- A double meaning often works well because the cleverness and wit stick in people's minds.

Match the tone of the name with the image you would like to project.

#24 GIVE ME A SIGN

Your sign is important. It is your hardest working employee. Your sign works 24 hours a day, seven days a week. It tells everybody who passes who you are and where you are. But is it letting your business down?

Is your sign in good condition?

- Is it faded, weathered, crackling or peeling? You are selling fresh fashion, so you need a fresh sign.
- Is it stable?
- Does it look professional?
- Is it easy to read? Is there enough contrast between the letters and the background?
- Are the color scheme and style current? While it is not generally

considered good practice to change the style of your sign on a regular basis, do check that it is current. You want your customers to know that you are up to date.

- How does you signage compare with other businesses around you?
- Do the colors catch your attention, or do they blend in with all the other signs in the vicinity?

#25 SIGN LANGUAGE

Cluttered signs can look a bit bargain-basement. The most effective signs are one to three words in length and usually no more than six words long. The message should be short, sharp and concise.

Your sign should be in keeping with your advertising theme, to optimize customers' recall of the ads for your business that they have already seen.

The rules of signs:

- Limit the sign to a few words, usually no more than six.
- Keep a contrast in color between the background and the lettering.
- Stick to one print type.
- Keep the print type simple (not fancy), so it is easy to read.

How much information should you put on your sign? Customers spend, on average, less than two seconds looking at a sign. So they need to be able to get the message in an instant. Use only a few words.

Remember: Keep It Simple, Sweetheart.

#26 PERSUASIVE

What are the most persuasive words?

Research has determined the most persuasive words in the English language are:

- you,
- money,
- easy,
- safety,
- save,
- new,
- love,
- discovery,
- proven,
- guarantee,
- health,
- results.

Others to add to the list are free, sale, now, yes, benefits, announcing.

Use these words, where you can, in your signs.

#27 A GOOD LOOKING SIGN

What makes a sign look good?

Pictures. As the saying goes, "a picture is worth a thousand words". Pictures are fast communicators and attention grabbers. If your sign is small, concentrate on the words and drop the picture.

Lettering style. Light lettering against a dark background or vice versa will give you a sign that is easy to read. The words need to be large and should be printed in a single font. Keep the actual lettering style clear. Avoid fancy, difficult-to-read fonts.

Colors. While color coordination is good for clothes, it is not good for signs. Maintain contrast in colors on the actual sign itself, and make sure that the signs do not blend into your existing decor.

No other signs. If there are too many signs to look at, the potential buyer will switch off. A bombardment of signs all competing for the customers' attention is the visual equivalent of shouting at them.

Correct spelling. Incorrect spelling does not make you look good. The only exception is if it is a deliberate play on words.

Punctuation is not necessary. Often a sign will not use a full sentence anyway. And punctuation can clutter the picture. Commas and full stops are not essential. The exclamation mark is good to use because it lends an air of excitement and commands the attention of the reader.

#28 CONSISTENCY

Keep the look of your signs consistent with the rest of your advertising, if you can. The sight of the sign while in the store will spark the customer's memory of previous advertisements, and that could land you a sale.

#29 POINT OF SALE SIGNS

If you need to place signs in your store, the best placement is that which interrupts the natural sightlines in a given area. Be the customer. Walk into your store and stand there. Take note of where you are looking. That is where you put your sign

Your point-of-sale signs are an inexpensive way to improve your profit. They:

- act as silent salespeople,
- direct the consumer to purchase.
- encourage impulse buying.
- plant the seeds for future buying.

Use them whenever you can!

#30 NEWS BULLETIN

Bulletin boards are an inexpensive way to remind patrons where you are and what you can offer them. They can be a very effective way of attracting the eye of the person who is "Just looking, thanks".

#31 WINDOW OF OPPORTUNITY

Does your front window do you justice? Does your window display say what you want it to say?

- Is the glass clean?
- Is it bursting with color and life? Or are you going for a restrained, chic understatement?
- Do you have posters in your window advertising what you can offer?
- Are there too many posters in your window that create a cluttered effect?
- Is the approach to the shop clear and inviting?
- Is the door easily accessible and easily seen? Is it clean?
- Do you have too many A-frame signs near the doorway?

Look like a boutique. Let people see the clothing style you offer and, if you sell accessories, be sure to dot a few in the window. When you hold a promotion, advertise it on a poster standing in the window. Choose a spot that intercepts customers' eye lines as they look in.

Ensure your window appeals to your target market. Does it reflect their taste? Does it reflect the image they want? Will they feel proud to be seen walking into the store? Is your decor mirroring the image of themselves they want to project?

#32 LET THERE BE LIGHT

Lighting should be bright enough to allow customers to see the quality of the clothing. Customers should be able to see the colors accurately.

It should not be so bright, though, so that the effect is sterile and unwelcoming. In upmarket boutiques particularly, a low light with spot highlights can enhance your quality atmosphere.

#33 MUSIC TO MY EARS

Music can be inviting. Or, if too loud or jarring, it can be off-putting. The right music often encourages the customer to stay in the store longer because of the ambience it creates. Sometimes customers will linger just to hear their favorite song if it is playing. And the longer a customer stays in the store, the better the chance they will buy.

The type of music you play will depend on your target market and the image you want your store to project. It must be age- and image-appropriate. If you don't bear this in mind, you might be doing your business a disservice. Happy music will help consumers enjoy their experience of shopping in your store. And if they enjoy being in your store, they will return.

#34 COMPLEMENT YOUR BUSINESS

Can you add other retail products that complement your fashion lines?

These are dependent on your target market and the positioning of your store in the marketplace. Choose items that 'fit in' with your clothing, as that is the mainstay of your business.

A women's store could offer accessories such as sunglasses, jewelry, shoes, hosiery, perfume, hair accessories, bags, purses and wallets, hats, lipsticks and nail polish, or underwear. Remember, your customer is here to spoil herself. You might like to carry an exclusive body moisturizer or accessories such as exquisite personal business card holders or elegant briefcases. The sale of these items will attract the impulse buyer or the person looking for 'something special', thus boosting your profit margins.

Conversely, are you stocking too many different types of items? If you spread your retail base too thinly you will clutter the store and confuse the potential buyer. Find a focus and stay within its boundaries.

#35 CROWDED HOUSE

If the customers can barely walk through the store without knocking things over, they will feel uncomfortable being there. Particularly if they have other parcels, strollers/prams or children with them.

Alternatively, if there does not appear to be much to choose from, customers will not return.

#36 ARE YOU UP TO DATE?

- Are your Christmas decorations still up in February? Take them down now!
- Do you have promotional advertisements in-store for upcoming occasions?
- Does your store look well maintained or does it have a tired, jaded, uncared-for feel? Ask a few friends for their honest opinion.
- Are your store decor items up to date? Wall hangings and pictures change style fairly rapidly. There's nothing worse than being able to date a business just by looking at the decor. Your customers won't have much confidence in your choice of fashion stock; they may not even enter a dated-looking store.

Check your business image once a year to keep abreast of fashion: don't wait to become so out-of-date that a huge overhaul is necessary. Not only is it more expensive, but you will probably have lost customers because of it in the meantime.

#37 CONSISTENT DESIGN

The interior of your shop should be a theme that is going to complement what you sell and create a positive atmosphere. Make sure the theme runs through the entire shop, and aim to stick to one theme at a time.

#38 STAND OUT FROM THE CROWD

There is a series of retail clothing stores in the same street, all carrying similar merchandise. Chances are that one will attract your attention more than others. You will choose one particular shop to enter first. What is it that makes you enter some stores and not others? The answer lies in the display.

How to display your stock is one of the most valuable skills your staff will acquire, since good application will bring sales and profits.

Mannequins and racks of clothes placed close to the doorway will capture the attention of the shopper; so will your window. Discount bins, specials and advertised new lines close to the doorway will help draw people in to browse. 'Special' signs, 'prompters', reminders of holidays and special occasions and the like are good attention grabbers. The strong use of color in the display, making the most of the items you sell, is always a winner.

Color and display are powerful attention grabbers. Of the five senses, it is the visual that attracts a whopping 87% of customers.

#39 GOOD BEHAVIOR

A customers' buying behavior once they are in the store can be related to their visual response. What you place on what shelves, and where, will affect the way a customer buys. The world's biggest super- market chains always place popular items-at eye level, for rapid turnover.

Statistics serves to highlight these facts. The third shelf on a gondola commands 32% of sales, with the fourth shelf attracting 23% and the second shelf 21%. Next comes the base at 15% and the top shelf at only 9%.2. It is amazing how unwilling shoppers are to look up, or to bend down, outside of their usual eye level.

So if you have shelving in your store it is wise to place your best selling items on the middle three shelves at eye level. Do not go against the grain, in an attempt to use these statistics to sell your slower-moving stock. It will not work. All it will do is tell customers that you do not have much good stock.

A way of tricking the customer's eye is to have shelves only at eye level. This way you are cashing in on the psychology of it all! Use the counters, use the walls behind the counter.

#40 TOUCHY FEELY

You have a clothing retail store and you need to display your stock. You could go around and study other stores and see how they do it. But how do you know which is the good way and which is the bad way? Read on, to save time and heartache of getting it wrong.

The first point to consider is that clothing is going to be worn. Your customers will want to see, feel, touch, unfold and examine before they buy. They need to be able to get their hands on your clothing range, enjoy the wonderful textures of the fabrics and test the color against their own skin.

Avoid placing clothes on shelves (unless of a fabric that is likely to droop or acquire hanger marks). Especially avoid shelves that are too high: customers need to be able to easily access their potential purchase. If it is too difficult or awkward, they will be turned off the purchase or, even worse, turned off your store.

If a flat surface is needed for display, tables are a better option than shelves. Be careful not to have too many. Place them away from the hanging racks for easy access. Ensure your customers, while bending over examining the items of clothing, are not bumping into the customers behind them at another table, doing the same thing.

But don't take everything off the shelves and tables and jam them all on the racks either! The clutter will turn your shoppers off. Have you ever tried extricating a tangle of coat hangers from your own too-full wardrobe? Can you imagine doing the same in a clothing store? It makes you angry and frustrated-you pull out other items along with the one you want, drop some garments on the floor. You battle with yourself over whether to leave the garment on the floor or drape it over the top of the rack. Neither situation is good for the store manager. Especially when the customer decides not to return to your store because she couldn't find what she wanted and didn't enjoy the shopping experience.

The ideal balance, is to have as many racks in the store as you can, without cluttering the floor space. There needs to be enough space for your customer to pull out a garment, hold it up to get a closer look, and decide to either buy it or try it on, or put it back on the rack. There needs to be enough room for your salesperson to stand with the customer-without crowding. There needs to be enough room for other customers to be doing the same.

At the same time, your store should be arranged so that looming empty spaces are filled with mannequins or accessories. Too much bare floor space will make the store look deserted. A busy shopper could retain an ill-perceived image of 'not much to choose from' and subsequently omit your store from her search.

#41 SHOP YOUR OWN STORE

Be the shopper in your own store, move around and see how it feels. Do the same in other shops. What feels good and what doesn't? The things that feel good, replicate in your shop.

#42 COMPETITIVE ADVANTAGE

Always be aware of your competitors. Find out what they do and how they do it. Then apply what they do to your business, but make sure you do it twice as well.

#43 IT IS YOUR BUSINESS

Remember you are in the business of helping your customers feel beautiful, well groomed and good about themselves. Everything about your store, from the design of your business card and invoice to the attitude of your sales staff, should reflect this.

CHAPTER SUMMARY

This chapter covered how to make your store look good and entice customers to visit. It covered:

- How to look the part from the inside
- What makes a good looking sign
- Your window of opportunity
- How to look the part from the inside

End of chapter two (2).

3 CHEWING UP THE PROFIT
Are your bad habits turning your customers off?

Your business is looking sharp from the outside and you have improved your sales techniques. You want to impress your clients. Have you considered that some of your mannerisms and your store behaviors might be doing your business more harm than good?

In this chapter you will find a list of habits that could be discouraging your customers from spending their money with you.

When you have finished reading this chapter, you should have an understanding of the following:

- Bad habits that could turn your customer off.
- Staff enthusiasm and how it affects your customers.

Time to change your habits!

#44 CLEAN AND ORDERED
Is your store clean and ordered at all times throughout the business day? It is not good enough to leave the cleaning and putting away until the end of the day. You never know when a customer will just walk in off the street.

Establish a routine where everybody is responsible for cleaning up after themselves. Try to get new stock unpacked as quickly as possible.

#45 WHAT IS THAT SMELL
Do you or your staff smell like a cigarette? This is a big turn off for most customers. Ensure staff do not stand around the front of your store smoking. If you or your staff must smoke, make sure this is done away from customers' view. Ensure hands are washed and breath is fresh before returning to work.

#46 DO NOT TURN YOUR CLIENT OFF

Are you turning your clients off? Here are some other things to avoid doing in front of customers:

- chewing gum,
- eating and drinking,
- using sloppy speech and grammar,
- telling dirty jokes; foul language,
- holding religious discussions and debates; and
- gossiping about customers and staff.

Ensure:

- your staff members are aware of these standards.
- you model them.
- you enforce them.

#47 DOUBLE NEGATIVE

Get rid of negative thinkers and negative philosophies. They have no place in your business and should never be allowed to come into contact with your customers.

#48 AN EXTRA PAIR OF HANDS

Are you understaffed? Are customers waiting too long to be served or even acknowledged when they enter your store? Would an extra pair of hands help? What about a free pair of extra hands?

By coordinating with schools and government employment training programs, you can use your store as a venue for the unskilled or for high school students to learn retail and people skills. There are advantages for both parties. The school or work skill organization gains a venue through which they can train people, and your business has extra staffing, for no monetary outlay.

Giving people the chance to work in your clothing store gives them the opportunity to learn valuable skills. You can train people in many areas of your business, such as:

- customer service,
- marketing developing newsletters , designing ads etc.,
- cash budgeting and management.

Such a scheme not only generates extra staffing but can also result in publicity and positive word-of-mouth for your business. If it is a school program (i.e. work experience or placement during school hours) you could even receive exposure in the school newsletter. Free advertising for you! If you do run such a program, be sure to let your local community newspaper know. They may want to profile your store, meaning more exposure for your business!

To run this program takes only a little of your time and some initial organization. You are also giving your time back to the community, which is a highly commendable thing to do. Your community backing is a sure way to bring the community's support back to your business.

#49 STAFF ENTHUSIASM

The attitude in your workplace greatly affects how the customers interact and whether they keep walking through the door. As Emerson said, "Nothing great was ever achieved without enthusiasm". The key is staff enthusiasm. Do they have it? Are they enjoying their job? Or is it merely something to pay the rent each week? What is their motivation? Are you encouraging them?

Staff need a reason to want to come to work. The solution is to make them feel important and valued, creating a sense of ownership of your business outcomes. Praise and reward them when all goes well, and offer constructive feedback when problems arise.

Set goals. Give staff something to strive for. Sales goals and targets that have rewards attached will create motivation.

Offer training and skills development. Your staff should feel as if they are the best equipped in their industry. Ongoing training also lets your staff see that they are important to the business and that their contribution is valued; it gives them a sense of pride and credibility in the job that they are doing.

Equipping staff and stimulating enthusiasm is something that will flow through to customers. Genuine enthusiasm is contagious.

#50 SHOW YOUR APPRECIATION

When your employees feel appreciated, they perform better at work. Providing meals for employees, especially when they work late, is always appreciated.

To motivate employees successfully, be sure you have clearly defined your goals and then use rewards and recognition to move towards those goals.

#51 FEEDBACK

Your employees need constant feedback and encouragement on how they are doing in their jobs. They need to be aware of their good and bad points and feel comfortable discussing work performance issues with you.

CHAPTER SUMMARY

This chapter covered the mannerisms and behaviors that might be doing your business more harm than good. It covered:

- Bad habits that could turn your customer off.
- Staff enthusiasm and how it affects your customers.

End of chapter three (3).

GROW
Increase the number of customers visiting your store

4 PAPER MONEY
Make money with direct mail, flyers, newsletters and business cards

Your business is looking sharp from the outside; you have improved you sales techniques and eliminated bad behaviors. Now it is time to get your name out there!

In this chapter you will find hints, tips and tricks on the following topics:

- Who to market to?
- How to market using flyers, newsletters and business cards.
- How to market using your invoice.
- How to personalize your marketing.
- How to stand out from your competitors.

Time to start getting your name out there!

#52 IN THE BEGINNING

Advertising, promotions and publicity is a waste of time unless you target it at a specific group (called a target market). Take time to select your correct target market. A clear vision of your target market will allow you to target your marketing and promotions to reach your most promising prospects.

Defining a target market will not limit your business. New business owners sometimes resist defining a target market, thinking it will reduce the number of potential customers. Not so.

Identifying target customers does not prevent your business from accepting customers that do not fit the target profile. If such a customer seeks your product or service, you will still be available. But you have not spent any time, effort or money in the hope that customer walks through your door.

How to Define Your Target Market

When you identify your target market you are simply identifying the specific characteristics of the people (or businesses) you believe are most likely to buy your clothes.

Common characteristics used to classify customers include:

- Age,
- Gender,
- income level,
- buying habits,
- occupation or industry,
- marital status,
- family status (children or no children),
- geographic location,
- ethnic group,
- political affiliations or leanings, and
- hobbies and interests.

Use these criteria to draw a profile of your target market.

There is nothing wrong with targeting two different types of customers. When you plan to target two different types of customers you can plan promotions relevant to each customer.

#53 TARGET MARKETS

Regardless of whether you have been in the industry for five years or five minutes, you should give a lot of thought to your customer profile and how you can reach these groups of people by means other than the traditional and expensive paid media.

The broad categorizations of clothing can be broken down into a number of segments, each of which have quite different incomes, needs and lifestyles. The categories are outlined below.

i. Teenagers, who fall into both working and non-working categories. Often teenagers fit the segment that their parents belong to, as their parents buy their clothes for them.

ii. Married working women aged 20-40 with no children. These are your classic DINKs (double income, no kids), with very high disposable income.

i. Single working women aged 20-40 with no children. Classified as SINKs (single income, no kids), again with high disposable income.

ii. Married or single women aged 20-40 with one or more children. Moderate disposable income and with vastly different lifestyle from the two groups above.

iii. Married or single non-working women aged 20-40, with or without children. Modest disposable income.

iv. Older women aged 40-plus. These women often have more leisure time and should be prime target markets, but might allow their shopping frequency to drop away for all sorts of reasons.

Having defined the above consumer groupings, is there some way that you can target these women other than by using conventional (and costly) media, such as television, radio and print? Think about your target market's lifestyle, and where they might go on a daily basis.

For example, you would expect to be able to network DINKs at country clubs, art galleries, restaurants, live theatre. If you frequent such places, talk to these people and let them know who you are and what you do for a living.

If you don't enjoy such networking activities, organize joint promotions with the establishments. Or you could place a few small, lower-cost advertisements in the appropriate club journals or theatre programs.

Women will be involved in aerobics and gymnasiums, craft and skills courses, dance classes, child care facilities and kindergartens, schools, junior sports clubs.

Senior women will have their own social venues, such as card clubs, senior citizens 'clubs, church groups, gardening clubs, bingo nights.•

No matter who your shop caters for, the theory remains the same. There are opportunities to leave flyers, hand out business cards or write articles for the organization's magazine or newsletter in each category and in each socioeconomic sector. Find out where they go and what they do and be hot on their heels with your marketing. You'll find that because you have directed your advertising to your specific target it will be much more effective-thus stretching your marketing dollar and making you more profit.

#54 WHY DO YOU PROMOTE?

The reason you promote your retail clothing store to gain more customers and retain them. So aim your promotions at customers you think you will be able to keep. Aim at the customers who will return, who will revisit on a regular basis, who will refer your services to others, and who will market your business for you because they, the customers, look good and hold reputable and prominent positions in the community.

Many customers will simply take the benefit of the promotion (i.e. the discount) and never come back. Some people skip from one store to another just to take advantage of a sale. This is a fact of life; it will always happen to some extent, no matter what you do. The trick is to minimize this occurrence. How?

Get the names and contact details of those who responded to the promotion and add them to your database. When you have done this, your promotion will achieve what it is designed to do:

- Not only will customers become aware of your store through your marketing, they will be given a reason to attend.
- Once they are in the door you have the opportunity to sell clothes and accessories.
- Having already met the new customer and provided them with service and garments, you now have reason to contact them again.
- Contact them-perhaps with the change of season-to thank them for their custom and notify them of new stock.

#55 RELEASE ME

A press release is one of the first publicity tools you should use. It is inexpensive, and when written correctly can be very effective. A press release is one of the better forms of advertising and marketing, as it presents you, your business or your product to the public under the guise of news, and it is free.

A media release is copy that you feed to the media in a newsworthy style, providing them with information they can readily print. Journalists may contact you to clarify details so they can write their own version. Your story can be used in print, radio or local television.

Send a press release to every magazine or newsletter that is connected or relevant to your business in some way. When planning a press release about your business, keep it simple, to the point, relevant and professional.

How do you write a press release? There are many free and paid resources available on the internet to help you write your first press release.

Too often people forget about creating their own publicity. Even more often, they don't realize they need to create their own. How often have you read the newspaper and wondered why other people's businesses seem mentioned so often? Why do they always get their photo in the paper when you don't? Have you ever wondered how the journalists know where the stories are?

The answer is in the media release. Contact the media yourself and you too will be in print. Journalists are always looking for stories. Each day they need new content to fill their newspapers and air time. So make it easy for the media, contact them first.

#56 ADVERTISING KEEPSAKES

Do you cut out and keep the ads you have placed in the newspaper and save them in a scrapbook? Great! But you should keep your own ads, and everyone else's, including your competitors'. Actually, you should keep the whole newspaper or magazine for future reference.

Quite often the proprietor and the advertising placer get into a routine because it is easy, safe and familiar. But is the ad actually working? Is it in the best position in the newspaper?

Look back and analyze your competitors' advertisements. How they advertised, what they advertised, and in what part of the newspaper they advertised. Now use the same criteria on your own advertisement.

Does the newspaper have an editorial section that could complement your business? Do your competitors advertise in these sections? Are their businesses successful? Is it worth following their lead?

If you advertise only spasmodically or for special occasions, buy the newspaper or magazine many times before placing the ad. Decide on the best placement for your ad. Note how other companies are advertising.

#57 BE DIFFERENT FROM THE OTHERS

Using the advertising keepsakes gathered above; note how your competitors are advertising. Then be different!

Use

- a different font
- a different layout
- a different orientation.

Your target market may not notice you simply because your ad looks like everyone else's or, worst of all, is being confused with your competitors' ads.

#58 ADVERTISING CHECKLIST

- Does your advertisement stand out, or do you have to search the newspaper to find it? For an independent opinion, try giving the paper to an unsuspecting friend who was not a participant in the design or placement of the ad.
- Does your ad have a similar look to other ads in the newspaper? Could your business be confused with someone else's?
- How does your ad look in comparison with your competitors'? Does it look like a poor cousin?
- Is it placed in a section that will draw your target audience? (E.g. near gossip columns and social pages)?
- Does the look of your ad reflect the style of your store and therefore target and attract the market you are catering for?

#59 BACK TO SCHOOL

Every parent who has a child at school knows they have to search their son's or daughter's school bag once a week to fish out the school newsletter. How many students are there at the local schools in your area? How many parents? How many homes and workplaces? How many relatives and friends do these people have? What a wonderful source of potential clients right under your nose!

Some schools provide a page where business owners may buy space by the semester to advertise on the back page or pages of their newsletter. If the schools in your area have already done this, jump onto the bandwagon. Once parents have visited your shop and were pleased with what they saw, you can be certain the word will spread. And it will be reinforced the next time their friend picks up the newsletter, only to see your ad.

If your neighborhood schools do not have this system in place, approach them and suggest they try it. Explain the advantages and income that can be generated by selling advertising space in their own newsletter.

Provide them with your business card to reprint, or design your own ad. Talk money, and they will probably acquiesce.

#60 DO YOU HAVE A CARD?

The business card can be one of your greatest marketing tools or it can be one of your greatest marketing wastes. The difference is how you put it together.

When designing your business card, highlight a slogan, mission statement or catch-phrase that sets your business apart from your competitors.

You need to give your card impact and visual appeal, to gain the customer's attention. Why?

A customer wants to telephone you, so they will need to thumb through a pile of small rectangular pieces of cardboard collected from almost every business establishment or service they have ever used. Do whatever it takes to stand out from this pile of cards.

Make sure your card does not look like everyone else's. If the business card looks good, different or special, it will earn a place on the refrigerator door. If it looks like just another business card, it will be filed in the drawer along with all the other business cards, or in the garbage.

Give your card impact and visual appeal. The fashion industry is a visual one. It is creative. Try to encapsulate the image and style of your boutique or fashion house in the design of your card.

A boring, conventional business card may not inspire your customers to visit your story. They might incorrectly perceive your store as old fashioned, simply from the impression created by the card.

#61 GIVE ME A SIGN

Your business card acts as a tiny sign. Be sure it catches the potential customer's attention and clearly explains the product or service you offer.

Your business card is sometimes the first contact potential clients have with your business, so make sure it is attractive, simple, and representative of what you specialize in.

#62 MORE INFORMATION PLEASE

Extra information can be printed on the back of the card. There is very little cost involved in adding further information on the back of the business card.

List your specialties, your services or your hours. List anything that will help sell your business and broaden your number of enquiries. But do not overload the card. Keep to your most important selling points while leaving the overall design simple and eye catching.

#63 COLOUR ME

When choosing the color of your business card do not go for a very dark color. Dark colors tend to inhibit people from jotting notes on the card about you or your business.

#64 CALLING CARD

If you decide to door knock to improve your business, you will need to leave a card. Or maybe a "Sorry I Missed You" note would be better. Mention on the back when you will next be in the area, and make sure you do go back on the specified day.

But why leave a small rectangular business card when you can leave something more interesting?

Your business card could be cut into an even more interesting shape, a dress or handbag, perhaps.

Maybe you could use a tag similar to the "Do Not Disturb" sign hung on hotel doorknobs, but with the words printed on it saying "Sorry I Missed You". And of course the name of your business, your address and telephone number appearing on the bottom.

#65 FRIDGE MAGNETS

Why not make your calling card and/or business card a fridge magnet. You could combine all of the above concepts and design a "Do Not Disturb/ Sorry I Missed You" tag in the shape of a handbag, shoes or dress, complete with a magnet on the back so it can readily be stuck on the refrigerator!

#66 FLYING HIGH

Flyers are an effective marketing tool. They can be dropped in mailboxes, handed out in the street, inserted in newspapers. Yet many fashion stores do not use them, because they think the flyers do not fit the upmarket image they are trying to project. But you can use the flyer and project your image.

The quality of paper and the color of the print will either add to or detract from the image you would like your store to project. So will borders, layout and illustrations. As a general guide, a spacious, understated layout projects class and exclusivity; a crowded flyer indicates bargains galore.

Be sure to use the colors that appear in your logo and your sign to reinforce your store's appearance in the minds of your customers. Do not vary the font used in your logo or sign just because it is now on a flyer. Keep the use of color, fonts and logos uniform.

Include an incentive for the customer to retain the flyer, and to come into your shop. An example might be to include a 10% discount on presentation of the voucher. However you decide to approach the topic of flyers, bear in mind your target market. Put yourself in their shoes, and give them something that represents your store.

#67 DRESS IT UP

Whether you distribute your flyer by handing it out to pedestrians or via a letterbox drop, you want to ensure that your flyer and your business name do not simply become part of a flyer collection, filed underneath a jar of biscuits in the kitchen or discarded along with all the other bits of paper that households accumulate.

An interesting way to dress up a flyer is to attach an attention grabber. One possibility is to use a real symbol of the clothing industry-a strip of fabric, a picture torn from a magazine, a tuft of cotton. A knitwear shop might staple a length of red wool to the flyer. To further arouse the potential customers' curiosity, add a headline that states:
KNIT YOUR OWN-OR COME AND BROWSE IN
KNITWEAR OUTWEST

#68 STAND OUT FROM THE CROWD

But have you wondered whether your flyer gets lost in a sea of other people's flyers and mail outs? Ensure it does not by making sure your flyer stands out from the crowd.

Study the examples you find in your own mailbox. Analyze the ones you get handed in the street. Avoid looking like all the other flyers. Especially avoid looking like your competitor.

Here are some tips.

- What color paper do the other businesses use? Try an alternative
- What print color? Use another.
- Do they have a picture? If they do, try going without- and vice versa.
- Is there an attention grabbing headline? This is a necessity for everyone.
- Is there too much information? Another important point for all flyers: do not crowd the space.

- Is there too little information?
- Have you provided a reason for people to patronize your store? Make sure you do!
- What size are the other flyers? Try a different size of paper.
- Does your paper have a fold? If so, make creative use of the fold try placing your attention grabber on the outside to entice the reader to open it and to read on. The word "FREE" printed on the outside fold will certainly create interest.

Good design in your flyer will ensure that these aims are achieved, and you will be on your way to making more profit.

#69 PUT YOURSELF IN MY SHOES

When designing the flyer, put yourself in the shoes of your customers. You know all about your business. Customers do not.

A well designed flyer will can:

- Catch the customer's attention;
- Help the customer remember who you are and what you do;
- Entice the customer into your store;
- Tempt the customer to buy while in your store.

#70 SPREADING THE WORD

A flyer is perfect if you have just opened the doors to a brand new clothing outlet or taken over an existing business, and want to get known in the district as quickly as possible.

Use eye-catching headlines and include the brand names or labels that you stock. Mention any special services your store has to cater for customers. Add the days and hours of trade. Your promotional offer could be a discount on your stock.

#71 SEEING DOUBLE

Double your advertising budget at no cost to yourself by negotiating a deal for cooperative advertising from your suppliers. If a supplier agrees to pay for half of the cost of an advertisement, then your available advertising budget is doubled.

Simply defined, cooperative advertising means your wholesalers or manufacturers agree to subsidize some proportion of your advertising. The percentage will vary from one supplier to another, so ask around.

The advantage to you is that it makes your advertising budget go much further, and you will also receive some high-level marketing guidance and direction from the supplier company.

The advantage to the supplier is that they get to have some control over how their garments are presented in the marketplace; they get to sell a lot more product; and they end up with happy and appreciative customers.

The best time to raise the issue is when you are being courted by a new supplier. Ask the company representative there and then whether the company is prepared to enter into advertising arrangements with you. If the answer is yes or even a qualified yes, ask them for details of how you could gain support and get them to put the details in writing for you.

If you already have a long-standing business relationship with your suppliers, by all means explore the topic with them. You've got nothing to lose and a lot to gain.

#72 BE DIRECT

Direct mail is a very efficient way to get your message out to prospective clients. That is if you can get people to read it! So how do you get your direct mail read? Make it stand out!

Everyone gets direct mail. Have a close look at some of the direct mail you receive and consider your own response to specific examples. No doubt you will find you respond differently to different ones. Are you having trouble deciding which direct mail is and which is advertising?

While both should have a target market, the way they approach the target market is what differentiates them. Advertising material is simply dropped in a letterbox. Direct mail is mailed to a specific individual, preferably by name, often by occupation. It will be labelled with an address, and sent by post.

Even direct mail can be divided into two groups:

- those addressed to a generic group of people, such as 'The House-holder', and
- those addressed to the person themselves, such as 'Jane Wilson'.

As a consumer, which form of direct mail would you be more likely to open and respond positively to? The psychology behind direct mail is that you will be more likely to read something that is addressed to you as an individual.

The effectiveness of direct mail is further enhanced by including personal details in the letter.

So how do you go about it? First, pinpoint the group of women you want to target. Take real estate agents, for example. Then send them a letter, something the one below.

Dear Simone,

In your job, you understand the importance of appearance. Street appeal, a fresh coat of paint and renovations will add to the value of a property. It's not just about buying a house, it's about buying quality.

You also understand the importance of your own appearance as a sales agent. People look to you for signs of success and amiability. An

34

uncoordinated appearance will not sell as well as a confident manner and easy style.

But you already know this. (Then you go on to mention the name of the boutique, the address, your name etc.)

Avoid the hard sell. Remember, you have chosen direct mail. Treat it with respect, just as you would write a friendly letter to an acquaintance. That includes your presentation. Choose high-quality paper and an attractive font.

Your goal is to gain more clients, so take steps to ensure that your direct mail has a higher chance of being read. Treat it as a letter. Include personal information relevant to the targeted individual. And remember, it is a different marketing tool from advertising. And it is cheaper.

#73 PUSH THE ENVELOPE

What makes someone open an envelope? People are more likely to open your envelope if it looks like a bill; if there is a hand written message on the outside; or if the outside teaser headline says that there is a free sample inside.

A plain white envelope can be effective. If it looks as if it has been dropped into the mailbox without a stamp, the receiver may think it is an invitation to a party rather than advertising material.

Other tips to get your direct mail read:

- Keep it fresh and do not bombard people with only one message. If they are initially interested, they might change their mind if you send the same flyer over and over again.
- Design a postcard style mail out.
- Simplicity is the key. The simplest designs can be the most effective.
- Be aware of postal restrictions. These may limit the size, shape and style of posted material. It is best to ask at your post office before you have anything printed!
- The message and envelope must be creative and have a focus. The envelope is part of the message in direct mail.

#74 MAKING HEADLINES

What is the first thing you read when you open a direct mail letter? The headline!

If the headline does not catch the reader's attention and entice them to continue reading, then you have wasted your money. The headline is critically important. The majority of the public reads little else when deciding whether or not they are interested.

Headline is 50% to 75% of the advertisement. The selling punch in your headline is the most important thing. It competes with news and articles and other headlines in picking out readers. Your single head line, in the average big town newspaper, competes with 350 news stories, 21 feature articles and 85 advertisements. And it competes in time, because, seen for a second, it is either heeded or passed up, and there is no return by readers'.

So tantalize the reader. Arouse their curiosity. Get them interested so they continue to read. Spell out the benefits of your business. Offer them something that you can give them. Some people read only the headlines. If they are pressed for time, the headline that offers the client something for nothing will entice them to read further. For example:

"$20 DRESSES" or "SALE ENDS SATURDAY"

Put any conditions to your offer in small print elsewhere on the ad.

#75 MARKETING WITH THE INVOICE

A cost efficient way to market your clothing store is to make all your paperwork multipurpose. What better combination is there than advertising your services on your invoice?

Invoices are not usually thrown away quickly, and some people never toss them out. Whenever your customer needs to know your phone number, or what your hours are or what exactly you offer, they will easily be able to find out the answers by looking at your invoice.

Use your invoice to value add your services:

- List the brands you stock
- Mention you stock jewelry, shoes, and/or bags.
- Mention gift certificates.

Whatever it is you do, print it on the invoice.

Once the client has your invoice, it will be studied now and the seeds will be planted for different future purchases. You may find your business growing because people know that you offer a broad base. And when someone asks "Do you know where I can get an outfit to wear to my daughter's wedding?" the name of your business will be on their lips.

#76 OUT OF THE BOX

Cut your advertising bills in half by doubling up on your mail outs. You have to spend postage on mailing out bills, invoices, reminder notices and thank-you notices, so mail out your advertising and promotional activities in the same envelope, including a hand-written note if it is appropriate. There is nothing like the personal touch to make people feel special-and your clients are no exception.

#77 CROSS PROMOTION

Increase yow- profits by cross-promoting your product. When wrapping a purchase, include a flyer in the bag promoting a new or related product. Place a catalogue of additional products you sell in bags containing your customers' purchases.

This will let them see your up-and-coming product lines before they come in again, and tempt them to buy more from you.

#78 PUT A NAME ON IT?

Have you ever been out shopping, carrying a bag with the name of a shop emblazoned on the side, and noticed that everyone glances at it as you walk by? Have you ever been stopped in the street by someone who has seen the name of a store on your carry bag to ask you where it was?

Putting the name of your store on the carry bag is a great marketing tool. Carry bags are mobile bill- boards.

As with all your merchandising and marketing, make sure the bag carries your store logo, using consistent colors and font. The bag should create the same image quality you want your business to convey. The instant recognition factor is important. You want a potential customer to see the bag as it walks past.

#79 READ ALL ABOUT IT

The newsletter is a great marketing tool for any industry, but it applies particularly well to retail clothing.

Your customers will enjoy reading your articles about fashion for the upcoming season, they will love to learn about the latest trends in accessorizing. They will smile over your news relating to your latest buying trip. Newsletters help you keep in touch with your customers. They show you care and that you know what you are talking about.

Make sure the newsletter is informative and newsy, avoiding a hard-sell approach. By all means offer information about your store and upcoming promotions, but present it in a soft-sell style. If your potential customers recognize an aggressive selling tone in your newsletter they are likely to throw the newsletter out, and all your efforts will have gone to waste. Bear in mind that you are trying a new marketing angle to attract customers, especially those who may not be won over by more traditional marketing styles.

One suggestion is to offer a newsletter or mini-magazine that is distributed quarterly, revolving around the four seasons. Include perhaps six to eight magazine-style articles or key features that relate to fashion. For example:

- Each quarterly edition could offer information on fashion for the upcoming season.

- Sell your summer and-spring clothing stock by cashing in on the outdoor entertainment season and the clothing required to make you 'look the part' and make the most of the warmer weather.
- Sell your autumn and winter stock by discussing activities in your area that relate to that time of year. Of course, your customers will need to be not only appropriately dressed but well-dressed to properly enjoy this time of year.
- Any festivities falling in that edition should be targeted. Your customers will need to be dressed appropriately for each occasion.
- Mention any sales coming up.
- Offer incentives for gift-buying seasons or occasions.
- Include articles that discuss projecting the right image in order to 'land that job' or even 'make men drool'.
- Include articles on self-esteem, as it relates to clothing.

Decide whether you will distribute the newsletter by letterbox drop or by posting to their mailbox. Posting direct, using the customer's name and address, would be the better choice, but you will need a database. If you do not have a database, get one! Without a database you are allowing your existing customers to wander into other stores. Once you've got them, keep them!

#80 NO BORES!

You want people to read your newsletters, so do not make them boring! It is important when writing newsletters to include human interest items and pictures, as well as the industry news.

#81 ADDRESS ME

Keep an address book on file of customers' names and addresses. You can then personalize your advertising, and keep your current customers loyal.

#82 GETTING TO KNOW YOU

Take the advantage of individually getting to know your customers; try to get to know what your customers want and need from business, then tailor your newsletters to suit them.

#83 THE PERSONAL TOUCH

Personalizing your communication with current and prospective customers substantially increase the response you get, without increasing your costs.

In the world of emails, a personal letter to your clients is a wonderful way to market your store. This is not direct mail. There is a difference. The direct mail letter is a generic letter that is posted to everyone and begins "Dear Customer". The personal letter mentions specific things that relate to that person alone, just as you would write a letter to a friend.

The personal letter mentions specific things that relate to that person alone, just as you would write a letter to a friend. This makes the customer feel you have been thinking of them and that you have been ordering items that cater to their individual needs and taste.

Avoid going direct to the hard sell. A more effective way is to follow up the initial personal letter with another, detailing specific promotions. This has the advantage of breaking the ice and opening the door to further business. You are setting up a relationship between yourself and the customer.

It is good to foster a feeling of kinship between you and your clients. Shopping for clothes is a personal thing, the customer often requires and values your input into her choice of clothing. Make use of this need and cater to it endlessly.

To be most effective, you can follow up the personal letter with another, detailing promotions. This has the advantage of breaking the ice, opening the door to further business. Avoid going directly to the hard sell, however refer to your previous letter.

The aim is to do the following:

- Gain the customer's attention first.
- Interest the reader with offers and benefits.
- Make reference to promotions that may be coming up.
- Put both the desire and the need to buy into the reader's mind.
- Tell the customer what they should do next: for example "Bring this letter in to Mary's Store before Monday the 31st to receive 20% of your purchase."

At all costs avoid making the letter look like a mass produced letter. The following list of tips will ensure your letter does not look like a mass produced letter:

- use the customer's name,
- add personal pieces of information that relate specifically to that particular customer,
- sign the letter yourself,
- include a hand written "PS" to personalize the letter even further, and
- use a warm tone, as you would to a friend, and
- hand write the address on the envelope

Big businesses are unable to market themselves in this way, as it would be cost inefficient for them. Make this your small business advantage. Customers will respond to the personal touch every time.

#84 STAY IN TOUCH

It is beneficial to establish relationships with customers through the entire year. Most customers will spend their Christmas gift dollars with the retailers they have established relationships with earlier in the year.

Another reason to keep in touch with the people your promotion attracted: they might tell their friends about you. Word of mouth advertising!

#85 THANK YOU

Send a hand written thank you note to your special/big customers.

CHAPTER SUMMARY

This chapter covered ways to promote your business and get your name out there. It discussed the following topics:

- Who to market to
- How to market using flyers, newsletters and business cards
- How to market using your invoice
- How to personalize your marketing
- How to stand out from your competitors.

End of chapter four (4).

5 MORE SALES, LESS BUDGET
Guerrilla marketing tactics

You may have employed many of the activities outlined in the previous chapter but your budget is running low. You would like some low-cost promotions to raise customer awareness of your business, generate more sales, and (hopefully!) increase customer loyalty.

Now it is time to release your inner guerrilla, guerrilla marketing that is!

Guerrilla marketing is when you use low cost, unconventional attention grabbing ways to draw attention to your business and products. It will help your business standout in the marketplace.

In this chapter you will find hints, tips and tricks on the following guerrilla marketing tactics:

- Directing traffic
- Gain celebrity status
- How to get edgy
- Making the good look better
- And many more promotions ideas.

Release your guerrilla now!

#86 LET'S HAVE A RELATIONSHIP

Why is it so important to have a relationship with your customer? Relationship marketing helps build customer loyalty. In many businesses the existing customer base tends to gradually erode as people drift away. Relationship marketing minimizes this problem.

Your relationship with your customers minimizes their tendency to switch to other stores. Relationship marketing does not have to be a formal concept of promotion. Rather, it involves getting to know your customers and letting them get to know you. Below are some easy ways to implement relationship marketing.

Let your customers know who your staff are

A simple way of achieving this is by providing name badges for your staff. Knowing the name of the person who is serving them can only help to build relationships.

Get to know your customers' names

When walking into a store there is nothing nicer than being treated with a consistently good attitude. And for the staff to remember their name from last time is a big thrill for the customer. The personal attention will keep them returning.

Talk to your customers

This is your best way to determine whether or not your service and facilities are meeting their expectations. Find out what they like what they like and what they don't like. Ask them from time to time how they think your service could be improved. Most importantly, put these improvements into action, if viable. This will let your customers know you value their opinion and their custom.

Feedback

To receive feedback from customers, use a suggestion bowl. Customers could write comments on the back of their business cards. An incentive for your customers to use their own cards could be competition-based. Or they may prefer the anonymity of blank cards, provided by you. The bonus for you is that you will build a database of clientele for future loyalty schemes. Best suggestion of the month could win a discount on their next purchase.

Good Manners

Above all, remember the customer is 'King'. Use those old- fashioned principles of good manners. Be polite and accommodating, and treat your customer the way you would like to be treated.

Encouraging feedback from your customers will help you draw conclusions about what areas your business needs to improve on. It's important to know how you can do more of what your customers like and want.

#87 WHY DID YOU STRAY?

Customers do not always stay with you. Sometimes they stray. It might be a fact of business life, but don't just accept it without a fight-or without at least asking why.

There are a number of ways you can approach this. You might like to contact the customers you have not seen for a while by sending them a letter or an email. Explain that, in the interests of continuing good customer service, you have included a questionnaire. Make the list as short as you can, but ask questions that will give you an insight into their feelings about your business. Some examples might be:

- What do you like/dislike about the physical appearance of the store?
- What do you like/dislike about our customer service?
- In which store do you most often find clothes you would like to buy?
- Is our store your first port of call? If not, why not?
- Include a stamped, self-addressed envelope and, as an incentive, offer a discount on their next purchase on receipt of the completed questionnaire.

There are many internet based survey systems you can use. Some are free and some are subscription based. A quick google search will find one that is right for you.

#88 WHERE HAVE YOU BEEN?

Customers change their buying habits for reasons that have nothing to do with your store. Customers change out of boredom, out of the need for a change. Or maybe someone else offered them a better deal. Haul customers you have not seen for a while back into your circle.

What do you do with friends you don't see often enough but would still like to keep in touch with? You drop them a line or a postcard. Treat your customers the same. Send them a postcard.

Choose a photo that illustrates your shop or print your logo and store name. Print shops have graphic designers who can manipulate existing photos. They have a huge selection of royalty free library photographs you can choose from

There are many software programs available and if your computer skills are not up to it, perhaps you could find a friend to help. There many services on the internet that will do graphic design, e.g. www.fiverr.com or elance.

You may choose to have your text printed on the card, but a handwritten postcard would have even more impact. Mention that the customer's presence in your store has been missed. Tell them about the new stock you have in store. Offer them a discount on their next purchase.

Once they return, make a fuss. Give them the red carpet treatment. Make sure they do not stray again. It is easier, more satisfying and much more cost-effective to retain old clients than it is to chase new ones.

#89 DRESSING UP THE STAFF

Many businesses want their staff in uniform. It identifies the staff as staff rather than customers, and it gives a corporate image to the business.

However, some styles of business do not call for a standard uniform look. Or perhaps the staff themselves are more fashion conscious and would prefer a standardized look that does not scream 'UNIFORM!

You have just found yourself a ready market. Approach these businesses by direct mail. Or perhaps you could contact the staff by telephone. Often the uniform decision is made by the staff themselves, and they just have to run the idea past their boss.

Offer a discount for a group purchase. Not only have you advertised the presence of your store, but you have set up possible purchases. Once the staff is in your store, they have a chance to see the range of clothing you stock, and the chance of selling other (non-work-related) items has increased.

Uniforms will need to change with the seasons of winter and summer. And often the fashion of the uniform itself will need to change every year or two. If you can secure the uniform business of several companies, you are well on your way not only to making more profit but to advertising your own shop at the same time.

#90 DIRECTING THE TRAFFIC

Is your store located upstairs in a shopping mall, or towards the end of an arcade? Do you find there is not as much pedestrian flow as you'd like? Then you need to find a way to bring your store to the people!

You will find in many cases that shoppers simply do not know where you are located. Either they haven't ventured in your direction before, believing there were no shops there that suited them, or the rushed shoppers chose not to waste time wandering around an area that didn't look as if it would serve them. As a consequence they are unwittingly avoiding your store.

A great idea is to hold a stall in a high-traffic area within the mall or arcade. Choose some items that are indicative of your style of stock. Include garments, handbags, and accessories. Choose the broadest spectrum that you can, to advertise your store. Make sure you have duplicates of the items in-store as well.

Customers might buy small items such as accessories from the stall, but garments will need to be viewed in a mirror, tried for size or examined in private. Do not provide a full-length mirror. Suggest to the customer that she might like to attend the store itself, where the same stock and more is sold. Tell her she will be able to decide on the item in peace and quiet, and gain a better view in the mirrors and change rooms. Make sure you put on the table a brochure or flyer advertising your store. Hand one to the customer. You have now redirected the traffic to your door.

A stall of this nature will pick up the customer who didn't know of your existence and will remind past customers that you still exist. It is not necessary to hold the stall on a regular basis. Do it periodically, perhaps every few months, to keep the name of your store and your stock fresh in the customer's mind. Choose reasons to hold the stall, such as Mother's Day or the first week of spring, and customers will respond positively.

A similar idea is to rent a window, dress it with your stock, and add directions to your store either in poster form or by brochures housed in a nearby stand. Often you can hire space in unleased store windows very cheaply, as center management are eager to fill in 'blank spots' in the shopping center.

#91 SOLD TO THE LADY IN THE RED DRESS

Combine a fashion parade with an auction, add a worthy cause, and you can have instant publicity for your store.

Many organizations are looking for novel ways to raise money for their cause, apart from selling raffle tickets. Approach organizations whose cause you personally support or whose members and affiliates might be aligned with your store. This is a terrific fund-raiser for schools and community groups.

Suggest the idea of an auction, where models would wear clothes from your store. This could almost double as a fashion parade. Provide your guests with a written program of garments with their label and a brief description-including the fact that they are available from your store. And, of course, you will be there on the evening, preferably co-compering with a representative from the fund- raising organization.

The venue could be a local club, with food and drinks provided in the ticket price. You will need to provide the auctioneer with a starting price, then the bids would go up from there. Or you could try a Dutch auction, where the price starts high and the bids go down. In this case you will need to tell the auctioneer the lowest price you will accept. It is at the auctioneer's discretion to thump the hammer at the bid he feels is reasonable, bearing in mind the suspense and the entertainment factor. He would know that it would defeat the 'fun factor' and the excitement level if he predictably sold the garment 'to the lady in the red dress' at the first bid.

The publicity spin-off from this concept could be huge. Publicity leading up to the occasion will help your business name and, of course, ticket sales. Photo opportunities in the local newspaper are a given.

#92 A NIGHT TO REMEMBER

Women love to shop. Women love to plan a day with girlfriends and shop. Women love to pour over fashion magazines to learn about style and to pick up some tips.

As teenagers these same women loved to get together to try on each other's clothes and work on combinations and accessories. So, why not make the most of it? Send out invitations to your current customers, ask them to invite all their friends and get them to come over to your store.

If you have the resources, ask someone in the fashion industry to host the night. Let them host some informal workshops to ensure your customers look their very best, every day of the year. Advice on 'key looks' for fashion and accessories would be mandatory, but perhaps you could gather together a band of style experts to expand the workshop into an 'event'. Imagine the impact on your customers and your marketing if hairstylists and make-up artists were also in attendance. Throw in a shoe-store owner and you've got it made. Your boutique will become the style mecca of town.

Be warned, you will move stock quickly! A group of girlfriends will encourage each other to buy items that look good. A lone shopper with a salesperson might hesitate over price, necessity and style, but when their girlfriends tell them how fabulous an outfit looks, they will believe them quite readily.

Add to this some style gurus helping the customer complete her look with accessories, and you will have some major sales on your hands.

The hairstylists will gladly give up their time because it will be a major opportunity for them to gain more clients. Haircuts will not be on the agenda on the evening, but advice will be. The focus would be on the latest looks for hair-those that complement the clothes currently in season. Other tips could include: how to modernize the styles the women are already wearing; what hair color suits them best; whether they should invest in foils, perms, extensions, straightening treatments; whether they should part their hair on the side, middle, or go without; whether they should opt for a shorter or longer style. The potential is enormous.

Likewise for the make-up artist or beautician. Make-up colors for the season, those that complement the outfits the customers try on, will be primary issues. They will then digress to skin and body treatments.

And what outfit is ever complete without shoes? Everyone in the fashion industry recognizes the importance of wearing the right style of shoe to complement the outfit. It is the shoes that pull the whole look together. So your colleague, the shoe-store owner, will bring a selection of styles and a handful of business cards-and they too will find customers knocking down the doors of the store the next day. (Obviously if your store stocks shoes, do not invite another shoe store!)

#93 MAKING THE GOOD LOOK BETTER

If you want to gain some new customers target some industries known for their love of clothes. Perhaps they need clothes for work, perhaps it is after-hours attire they are looking for. It does not matter.

Who you invite would depend on your target market. Invite the people who have a need for the type of clothes you sell. You could try:

- professional offices-accountants, lawyers, marketing,

- an art gallery director and her staff.

Write a follow-up letter to each of your guests after the promotional evening. Thank them for the pleasure of their company and mention that you will be in touch to tell them when the new stock arrives.

#94 EXTRA EXTRA

To add to the excitement of the shopping evenings and give the shoppers a little extra, you could offer a discount. You might all contribute to a prize package to be won by one of the workshop participants.

Supply drinks and some snacks, and your customers will have a fantastic night. And because the atmosphere is so encouraging, they will spend their money then and there. A promotion will keep working long after the evening is finished.

You could hold your workshops immediately before every season-and you might find that customers will delay making their purchases until the anticipated event. After all, it is better than making fashion   blunders and throwing money away on unsuitable items.

#95 A MAGICAL MYSTERY TOUR

Apart from necessity and a sense of fashion, why do people buy clothes? Many women shop as a form of entertainment.

When there is nothing to do, some enjoy wandering around shopping malls, others meet friends for lunch in one of the shopping centers then peruse the stores; some plan all-day shopping trips with friends and family.

Take advantage of this idea, get together with other businesses, and organize a shopping tour. It could be run twice a year, and once it has been organized the first time, the subsequent times become easier.

Boutiques, shoe stores, jewelry stores, coffee shops and restaurants could all get together. The tour organizer would need to approach targeted stores to see whether they would participate. All participants would then collectively choose one of their slowest trading days to hold the tour. A bus company would need to be approached and an agenda of outlets drawn up. You could break up the shopping with morning tea or coffee at a cafe and lunch at a restaurant.

Depending on the size of your town, different levels of tours could be organized according to budget. More exclusive boutiques and restaurants could be included on one tour, and moderately priced fashion houses and eating places covered on another. You could advertise the event by providing flyers in participating stores, or by letterbox drop, or both.

Properly organized and promoted, these buses can be pre-booked and filled to capacity. Mothers' groups, or groups of older women, might be interested in a day's outing, and might look forward to a day of shopping with friends, especially if you organize child care.

A promotional concept such as this has many benefits:

- you are once again raising the profile of your store in the mind of the public,
- you are drawing more customers through your doors, and
- you are increasing your chances of making sales.

This type of day has the added lure of allowing customers to plan ahead, perhaps putting off other shopping expeditions because they have committed themselves to the day of the promotion, so they'll tend to save up for the day.

A fun outing with a group of friends puts the shopper in a happy frame of mind. And happy people buy. Your shop will be associated with good times in their mind from then on.

#96 CORNERING THE HARD TO BUY FOR MARKET

Buying presents can be difficult, so make it easy for your customers. Offer a gift certificate.

The idea isn't new; it's tried and tested. But there are some points to bear in mind.

Promote the fact that you have gift certificates. Post signs in the window or on the counter to remind your customers. Sometimes people desperately need to buy a present but have no ideas. In these cases, particularly if they are strapped for time, it is the item that catches their eye at that time that will win their dollar.

Make the certificate **look good**. Make it look stylish. This is for the benefit of both the buyer and the recipient of the gift. The buyer will be more tempted to purchase the voucher if it is attractive to the eye. On opening the card, the recipient will be more pleased to receive a beautiful certificate with which she can redeem her goods.

The voucher might be shown to friends, stuck with a magnet onto the refrigerator, where others will see it, before the clothing is collected. And an idea for future purchase of a certificate, by the receiver herself, has been planted.

Be aware that some unscrupulous individuals out there are scanning gift vouchers into their PCs and manipulating dates or recreating identical certificates. Here are some to tips to avoid this:

Use distinctive paper, a stock not readily available, or get a plastic gift card

- Hand-write at least some information on your voucher and sign it.
- Use a distinctive-colored pen.
- Keep a record of all vouchers given out-who bought them, and for whom.
- Number each voucher and tick them off when they are redeemed.

#97 BLAZING A TRAIL

Remember Little Red Riding Hood, innocently picking flowers on the way to Grandma's house? Well, be the Big Bad Wolf and lure Little Red Riding Hood off her path!

- Post teasers in the street at intervals, to catch people's attention and direct them towards your door.

- Post a 'thought of the day' or 'thought of the week' in your window or on the A-frame sign in front of your store-or even on posters in the street.

- Write a quick note about current fashions or stock and do the same thing.

- Find some quotes from well-known fashion designers or models and write them on posters or billboards. Be sure to change them often.

- Devise an ongoing comic strip that can be taped to your window-even better if the theme of fashion can be worked into the story. Think of your own life, add in a bit of spice from other people's lives, and you have an instant soap opera. And what does everybody know about soap operas? You get hooked!

The sagas of the main character could   involve romance, parties, the races, that dinner party disaster, anything that could revolve around social occasions and fashion. It could be as serious or as comedic as you like. The sky's the limit, the topics are endless. Have fun doing it and watch new customers come to enjoy the story, and your old customers return to see the latest. If you don't feel confident enough to style the cartoon yourself, approach a local art or design student who might be grateful for the exposure. At the very least, it's a talking point for any customer who comes through your door. And selling is all about opening up the channels of communication. And to top it off, they'll tell all their friends about it.

So create your own publicity, attract customers by other means than the usual 'SALE' sign. This kind of approach will lift your 'dead spots'-those times of the year when retail sales are down.

#98 PACKAGE DEALS

Everyone loves a package deal. It works for the tourism industry. There's no reason it can't work for a retail clothing store. The tourism industry uses package deals to lift their sales in the off season. Use the same way of thinking to increase your trade during your quiet periods.

You might like to look at a time of year-or perhaps extend the concept to a particularly quiet day or night of the week.

- Hook up with a florist, music store and wine shop outlet close to your premises.

- Each business offers a discount to lure the customers in.
- Share the printing costs of flyers.
- Distribute the flyers and nominate the night or week that the package is available.
- Tick the box that relates to your business, date and stamp it, and get all the associated businesses in the package deal to do the same.
- Customers must have bought the goods within the agreed time frame to qualify for their discount from each store.

If customers choose to buy from your business only or maybe only one of the others, forgoing the complete package, it doesn't matter. You have still cut your printing costs and got your name 'out there', and you have still given your business the opportunity to make a sale.

#99 SHARING COSTS

Most proactive business owners distribute flyers and brochures to advertise their businesses. They do this because it works. But why pay for all your advertising alone, when you can share the costs with others?

Get together with other retailers and service industries and share printing costs. You might decide to print your business on one side of the paper and your colleague's on the other. You could divide the paper horizontally, vertically or diagonally and share halves that way. Of course, you could divide the paper between any number of businesses!

Marketing your business this way creates a win/win situation:

- Printing and distribution costs are reduced, increasing your profit.
- Because of this you might be able to advertise more often.
- You have the chance of gaining customers from your colleague's complementary business.
- The chances of your flyer being retained are greater.

Getting your business name out there + sharing printing costs while you do it = more profit!

#100 WELL DONE

Everyone likes achievers. Everyone likes associating with achievers. And, as the motivational gurus say: "Surround yourself with achievers and positive people and you will become one yourself".

So scan the newspapers for individuals in your area who are on their way to success. Choose the big guys or, for an easier path to their doors, target those who have been recognized but who have not yet been thrust into the highly competitive world of marketing and sponsorship. It does not matter whether they are known for their musical achievements, their sporting prowess, their theatrical abilities or their business acumen.

Send them a congratulatory note or card praising their achievements and sign it, printing the name of your store on the bottom. Include a discount on their next purchase to entice them into your store.

#101 CELEBRITY STATUS

Have you noticed how people follow the advice of so called gurus?

If Revlon or Bobby Brown say 'Pink is in', everyone flocks to the make-up counter to buy pink lipstick. If a society hairdresser decides the new look is short, neat and gelled, scissors all over the world start snipping at long locks. If Ralph Lauren or Donna Karan mention the word 'bohemia', smart-suited women all over the world suddenly adopt loose- fitting, flowing, bespangled garments. Why? Style gurus are people whose experience, history and talent are known to everyone. They enjoy an elevated status.

What can you learn from this? Elevate yourself. You may not have the paparazzi and magazine journalists hounding you or hanging on your every word, but you have the ability to create your own celebrity status within your own com- munity. Pretend you're famous and everyone else will believe you.

Start with the layout of your newspaper or magazine ad.

- When you place your ad in the newspaper, try pushing yourself to the forefront. Name your store after yourself. Choose a name of strength if you want to achieve this type of image. A first name followed by a surname works well.

- Place your name or your store's name on the left-hand side. Underneath this, give yourself a spiel. Mention the labels you stock. State your dedication to personal service. And then offer a discount as an extra motivator.

- Top it all off with a photograph of yourself on the right- hand side with a current hairstyle and outfit.

And remember, keep running the ad. Readers will assume you have status. There will be no reason to think otherwise. This is exactly what the marketing machines do for movie stars and reality stars!

#102 BE A GURU

Why not become a fashion guru yourself? Build up as much 'front' as you can. Adopt the manner of a guru-someone knowledgeable in your field.

Approach your local newspaper to discuss inserting editorial comments or even a regular column where you can write about topics centering on fashion, self-confidence and grooming.

You could choose a different topic relating to fashion each week, written in an informative style. Look to the glossy magazines to give you some ideas. Or perhaps you would prefer a more relaxed style of writing, relaying information in an anecdotal manner.

There are many benefits to producing editorial for your community newspaper. No matter which format you choose, it is advertising that doesn't really appear to be advertising.

You get your own name and your business name in print. You might even get your photograph attached to the column. And the article says more about your expertise than any advertisement could: it elevates you to 'guru' level in your field-and that will give your boutique a more solid public image.

#103 CARD GAMES

You designed some super special business cards that are eye-catching, specific, clear and effective.

They have your business name, specialty service, address, e-mail address, web address and phone number. Now what to do with them? They can be your best guerrillas.

Spread them!

Business cards are your little business advertisements, and you want to spread them around to get noticed. Talk to libraries, supermarkets, office blocks, businesses campuses etc.-in fact, anywhere there are people!

Ask at hospitals, dentists' and doctors' offices too. Ask whether you may post your cards on their notice boards, in their bathrooms, or in other areas where they will be seen. Be creative: anywhere is good as long as your prospective clients can see it.

Pass out

Your business cards are no good to you while you are holding onto them. Do not pass up any opportunity to hand out your cards to other people.

Did you buy petrol this morning? Leave your card. Did you go to the shops to buy groceries? How many cards did you leave, either with individuals or on the counter?

If you do not think the people shopping in your area are interested in your services, then shop where your clients do. Infiltrate your target market and get to know their habits and preferences.

Paid any local bills by mail lately? Did you include your business card in the envelope? Perhaps the person opening the mail will need your service or know of a friend who does. Do not waste an opportunity to get known, as every encounter has the potential to generate more profit for you.

#104 SOMETHING FOR NOTHING

You have heard how valuable word-of-mouth referral is. The problem is that not all clients will run around the local neighborhood voluntarily, raving about your store, no matter how good you and your staff are. The simple reasons for this are: they were never asked; or the idea did not even occur to them.

You can overcome these short-term impediments by actually asking your satisfied clients whether they would mind providing you with a testimonial. Be sure to explain to them carefully how and where their testimonial will be used.

You may simply want to write their quotation on a sheet of butcher's paper and post it in a window. Or you might want to carry the idea through to flyers, letters or even into the mainstream media.

Most people will be delighted to have their comments published. You could even change the testimonial so regularly that it becomes a marketing gimmick. It could take on the same tone as a soap opera, where the locals tune in to see who has been to your business lately and to find out what the latest one has said. This can add a bit of fun to the process and takes the heat off one or two clients, making them more likely to agree to participate. You could even find it takes on a life of its own, as competitive nature kicks in, with some individuals clamoring for their 15 minutes of fame!

Even those who say no will be flattered that you asked them anyhow. Often they will come around with a little gentle persuasion; if not, they will enjoy telling their friends the story. And that is more publicity for you.

There is now a group of satisfied customers who are happy to say nice things about your business and its staff. It is free, and it is good for your business.

It is important that you do not pay for testimonials or for their subsequent use. The whole point is people voluntarily recommending your business, without being paid. They are going to do it for nothing because it is flattering to them, because it is the truth, and because they know that every time they return for an appointment you and your staff are going to give them extra special care and attention.

#105 WORD OF MOUTH

Customers can become your cheapest and most effective form of advertising. Treat them well and your business will benefit from their positive word of mouth.

#106 LAUGH YOUR WAY TO MORE PROFIT

Creativity and humor go hand in hand. An injection of humor could well see your sales increasing.

Humor has a feeling of rawness, of honesty. And honesty is a virtue that every merchant wants to promote in relation to their business. Honesty wins customers' confidence. Honesty sells.

Humor can be used in your business in many ways. For example:
- your uniform
- your car

- your happy-go-lucky manner
- your mail outs
- your newspaper ads.

#107 STAFF THINKING

Encourage and reward open and creative thinking from your staff. Not only will you get a greater range of ideas, but the staff will feel as though their opinions are valued, enhancing job satisfaction and reducing voluntary turnover.

#108 THE NOTEBOOK

Always be on the lookout for new, impressive ideas you could adapt to your business. Keep a notebook with you, to jot down the ideas as soon as you spot them. When it comes time for brain storming promotional ideas, refer to your notebook.

CHAPTER SUMMARY

This chapter discussed how to release your inner guerrilla, guerrilla marketing that is! It covered the following guerrilla marketing strategies:

- Directing traffic
- Gain celebrity status
- How to get edgy
- Making the good look better
- And many more promotions ideas.

End of chapter five (5).

6 SMALL COST, BIG IMPACT
Get noticed on a small budget

OK. So you have done the newspaper ads, the posters in the windows, the A-frame at the front of your shop, the business card. You know you need to drum up more attention, but the cost of more advertising seems out of your league. Do not let that stop you!

Getting noticed does not take a big budget. You do need to be creative and available, to realize the opportunities that are out there.

In this chapter you will find hints, tips and tricks on the following low cost ways to promote your business:

Making your mark
Joining forces
Winners are grinners
Attention seeking tactics
Freebies, and
Frequent buyers.
Start getting noticed now!

#109 MAKE YOUR MARK

OK. So you've done the newspaper ads, the posters in the windows, the A-frame at the front of your shop and a good business card. What else can you try?

You want something that will be kept, not thrown out in the rubbish. You want a memento that will not cost the earth. How about a bookmark? You can hand bookmarks to your customers at the end of their transaction. You can keep a stack of them on your counter. You can hand them out as you would a flyer, or include them in direct mail outs.

Design your own, adopt the ideas of a graphic artist, or combine the two perspectives and take the artwork to your local printer. The basic ingredients are a rectangular piece of cardboard and a hole punched in one end with a ribbon threaded through and knotted. Be sure to tell the designer and printer your budgetary requirements, because the type of card and its thickness, the number of colors used, the style of the design and extra features such as metallic paint will all influence the cost.

To maximize effectiveness, the layout and color scheme should be consistent with the colors of your logo. If your budget allows it, your printer will also print the name of your store on the ribbon itself. Your job is simply to cut the ribbon into lengths and thread it through the hole.

What you put on the bookmark should be consistent with the image of your shop. For example, a jeans shop catering for the youth market will need a contemporary look. An upmarket, conservative boutique will need a classier bookmark.

An extra reason for clients to keep your bookmark might be the inclusion of information consistent with fashion. List styles of clothing flattering to each body type. Mention fashion looks for the coming seasons. Include the latest accessory styles. Add make-up and hairstyles that complete the current fashion look. Or print a quote by a fashion icon, such as Coco Chanel.

An idea could be to print a series where the fashion tips are all different, to encourage customers to collect and keep the bookmarks. Or you could continually update the tips, once each batch has been distributed.

Of course your shop name, address and phone number will be prominent .You might also like to include your opening hours, the services you provide and the labels you sell.

#110 HAPPY BIRTHDAY

As children, we all looked forward to our birthdays. Not only were we a year older but, more importantly in our eyes, we looked forward to the deluge of presents has usually dropped off dramatically.

How can you, rectify this situation? Make your regular customers feel special again, and offer them a gift from your store.

Use your database to access your customers' birthdays. They may not want to give away their year of birth and that is ok. You only need the day and month. Send them a birthday card and include a certificate offering a discount on their next purchase.

Make a fuss of the customer when they enter the store, and ask about their birthday celebrations. You might even like to keep a stash of wrapped fruitcake on hand, and give them a slice after the transaction has been made.

The benefits of this type of promotion are numerous:

You are sending out flyers to promote your business and to remind your customers to return to your store.

This is not perceived as random advertising, which some customers might tend to ignore. You have targeted a specific customer, with a good reason to send out the flyer in the first place.

The customer will be pleased to be remembered by you, lifting their perception of both you and the store itself.

They will return to your store to receive their discount and perhaps find something else to buy.

The customer will be thrilled with the idea and will hopefully tell all their friends.

Personal attention is one of the most effective ways to retain your customers and win new ones. Many stores nowadays concentrate heavily on moving stock and increasing turnover, regarding customers as walking dollar signs. If you can show your customers you are thinking about them at a personal level, they will return to lap up the attention.

Everyone likes to feel special!

#111 KEEPING IT IN THE FAMILY

When you have secured one member of the family as a customer, it makes good marketing sense to target other family members.

A women's clothing store could align sisters. As owner of the store, you might nominate a new occasion, not Mother's Day but Sister's Day. Allocate your own day of the year and run a promotional campaign announcing your fabricated selling occasion. Choose a time of year that is traditionally low in retail sales. Both sisters would need to attend on the given day for both to receive a discount on purchases over a set amount.

Ask your customers to fill out a form giving their date of birth, address and style preferences, and keep them on your database. Now you can keep in touch with them for marketing purposes.

Depending on your target market, your range of stock and the impact of the generation gap, you could extend this family purchase to mothers and daughters. This promotional idea could work particularly well around Mother's Day. When the daughter buys an item of clothing from your store as a gift, she receives a discount on a purchase for herself.

The idea behind these suggestions is to extend your customer base and to catch more sales. In the process, you are generating more publicity for your store. If your store is situated in a mall, throw the idea to center management to work up a retail promotion. Centre management is always looking for promotional ideas, and might welcome a 'Sibling Saturday'.

#112 JOINING FORCES

What one thing common to people the world over makes them smile and sends a little tingling sensation through their body? Getting something for free!

"But how can I give away stuff from my store?" you ask, "I'll go broke!" The solution is easy. You give away stuff from other people's stores.

Think about cross-promotional opportunities with colleagues in complementary businesses. What kinds of business would like to associate with a women's clothing store? The list could be very long. Here are a few: restaurants, fashion stores, wine stores, chocolate shops, lingerie stores, home ware stores, linen houses, florists.

Would the chocolate shop owner be prepared to offer your clients a two for the price of one deal if you directed 100 or so customers to their establishment? Would they be interested in offering their chocolate loving patrons a discount on clothes at your establishment?

Think of photographers. Would they offer a discount price on the cost of a sitting?

If your business is located in a shopping complex, try to make friends with retailers in neighboring shops. You can exchange promotional ideas and create complementary advertising campaigns.

#113 BE ATTRACTIVE

Get smart. Show off your stuff. Let people what you have got and what you do. Being in business is not the time to be timid. Shake off any shadows of shyness.

How can you attract attention?

Use your car. You are driving around in a mobile billboard sign. Use this to your advantage. You already have to travel from points A to B, so it does not cost a cent more to get out there and let people see your name. Think of it as getting your name up in lights. It may not be Broadway, but it certainly is your own show, so it is up to you to make it work.

Get a good-quality sign made up and attach it to your car, remembering to include your business name, telephone number and a brief headline of what you do, your specialty service or approach. If you are not able to attach a sign to your car, then consider the magic of magnetic signs-magnets will do the same job without any hassle. Now do not forget to park your car in places where it will be noticed, and keep it tidy!

Make friends. Join up with compatible businesses in your area and agree to refer clients between you.

#114 WINNERS ARE GRINNERS

There are many organizations that run raffles. And every raffle needs a prize. What better way to advertise your boutique or clothing store than by donating a raffle prize?

Post a sign near your cash register mentioning that you would be happy to donate a prize for fund-raising raffles. Limit the value of the prize to something you feel comfortable with. Ask that the name of your shop be printed on all raffle tickets, and specify that you would like to be present at the draw to choose the winning tickets. Request also that there be a photograph in the local newspaper, featuring you with the smiling winner.

Image the advertising you have bought for the price of a new outfit!

The organization is paying printing costs to feature the name of your store on their raffle tickets.

The name of your store is being disseminated throughout the community on each ticket that is sold. Even people who don't buy a ticket will hear the name of your shop as sponsor.

Your presence at the draw will mean you are able to market yourself and your shop and meet more potential clients.

Photo opportunities in the newspaper are a highly sought-after form of advertising. What better form of print advertising can there be than one that is distributed so extensively in the community, and at the same time is free? In addition, it is not perceived as advertising by the majority of readers, as it appears under the guise of 'news'.

The winner has great potential to become a new client. They must come in to your store to choose their prize, so that's another person in the door- and you can bet that in their excitement they'll be telling all their friends about their win and their impending shopping spree.

Add to that the fact that whenever they wear your outfit and people ask where they got it, the name of your store will be on their lips. Thrilled to have won something, they will probably volunteer the information without even waiting to be asked! This approach brings the possibility of winning not just one new client, but hundreds more. And imagine the potential for advertising your business if you donate to more than one organization.

Study each request for donations or support to see whether it is something in which you believe strongly. Is it a legitimate cause? Is it too controversial and might alienate your customers?

#115 ATTENTION SEEKING TACTICS

Why do not you try the following?

Talk: Volunteer to speak in your area of expertise to interested groups. Do not try to sell anything, just be there to spark people's curiosity. This is easier than you may imagine at first.

Think about your target market, the people you would expect to be your clients. Where do these people go for relaxation and recreation? What are their hobbies and interests? What clubs and societies would they belong to? Now, within these areas there will undoubtedly be groups, clubs and societies that host information evenings or social events. Get involved.

Most often there are groups just dying for a speaker. These are captive audiences for you and potential customers. Think laterally and cast the net wide.

Consider library and book groups, sports groups, business lunch groups, mothers' groups and nursing homes/homes for the aged. Even if these people are not interested in your services themselves, they will have friends and family members who might be. People will talk, and this is great for business.

Write: Approach your local newspaper or suburban magazine and offer to write a weekly column on your area of expertise. Also consider local radio and regional television stations: they are often looking for experts to host and present topics of interest. Offer to do this free. Remember, this is your advertising budget and it is many, many times more valuable than what you would otherwise have paid for. Make your article or session informative and entertaining. Do not do the hard sell here. What you are doing is establishing a fantastic reputation for yourself so that clients will be drawn to you.

Network You have heard it before, you have done it before, but the word still sounds a little scary. Relax! You know what you have to do, join groups and talk to people. Contact your local chamber of commerce or industry association and identify local businesses and groups you might be able to target.

Call the contact person and explain what you do and what your interests are, always considering how you could complement and help each other. Look up the "Clubs" section of your local telephone directory and make a few telephone calls to the club secretary; find out when their next meeting is and go along as a potential new member. Join if you can but make sure the group is worthy of your investment before you sign on. Remember, you are not there to sell your services directly; you are there to make friends and contacts.

Make sure you go armed with an excellent business card. Hand out your cards at every opportunity.

Each time you meet a new person, hand them a card and introduce yourself. If a conversation results, and it probably will, this is your opportunity to market yourself and your business. Take advantage of it. Work out beforehand what you will say and what points you want to get across. Prepare a 30-second introduction, outlining who you are, what you do and how your business benefits others. Remember, people tend to do business with people they know.

#116 FREEBIES

Everybody loves a freebie. But offer your low-cost freebies along with a customer purchase. Do it whenever you can, but always with an ulterior motive in mind. Let them take away a gift that will advertise your business.

Here are some ideas:

Free telephone and address books, jotter pads, business card holders, post-it notes-all with your business name, address and phone number beautifully inscribed after purchase.

Give free designer T-shirts bearing your stylish logo. This would depend on the size of your business and your resources. Select key individuals in your community, or customers who buy from you on a regular basis or who have made a particularly large purchase. You might even find that your T-shirts become highly sought-after and that you are able to sell them if they are tastefully done. Esprit used this marketing tool to perfection.

Run a competition and give away a gift voucher for:

The Best Mum-for Mother's Day,

The Best Grandmother,

Teacher of the Month,

Secretary of the Month,

Most Caring Nurse.

The list is endless. Nomination sheets can be available from your store, your social media sites (more on this later), or in the local newspaper. Make the most of the competition with a photo opportunity in the local newspaper.

A picture of you presenting the best secretary or teacher with a stylish new outfit, with a smile or a kiss on the cheek, is great publicity.

#117 KEEP IT USEFUL

If you are going to invest money in merchandise advertising your business name with the specific purpose of giving it away free in a promotional special, make sure the product is going to serve some use to the customer. If it does not they will throw it away, and you lose your money.

#118 FREQUENT BUYING

Most people are familiar with the frequent buying (or loyalty) system. The concept is an oldie but a goldie, and is worthy of mention. All retail and service industries have found that those who sign up on the frequent-buyer program increase the rate at which they purchase. In addition, it reduces defection to other businesses.

Why does it have such strong customer appeal? Get something for nothing. For example:

Buy 8 items of clothing, next purchase receives 10% discount

When customers are approaching purchase number eight, they have a strong incentive to buy their next clothing item from your store. You might even find that just the discount encourages that next buy.

Loyalty schemes reduce impulse buying of items from other stores and direct customers' thoughts to your boutique. So they are discouraged from buying that little blouse that catches their eye as they walk past a neighboring shop. They know they are on their way to receiving a discount at your store, so they will make the extra effort to get there first.

There are many resources online for managing a loyalty scheme. You will be sure to find one that suits your store.

#119 BECOME A VIP

Everyone likes rewards. As children, we liked to receive a pat on the back, a gold star or a special treat. As adults, nothing has changed.

Reward your regular customers. Make them feel special. Make them feel welcome. Make them VIPs. And give them a card that says so.

Awarding VIP status at your store recognizes the customers' value not only to you but also to themselves.

Of course, part of being a VIP is receiving a 10% discount. Customers will feel important and receive a discount too!

But do not hand out the cards indiscriminately or they will lose their importance. Save them for the regular customers, the big buyers, or for your initial customers if you have just opened a new store.

Make the card look important. Print the letters VIP in large gold lettering on the front of the card. On the back, print:

(Insert name) is entitled to receive a 10% discount on purchase at (name of your store). Then sign it personally.

CHAPTER SUMMARY

Now that you have finished this chapter you should have an understanding of the following low cost ways to promote your business:

Making your mark
Joining forces
Winners are grinners
Attention seeking tactics
Freebies, and
Frequent buyers.

End of chapter six (6).

7 MAKE MONEY ANSWERING THE TELEPHONE
Telephone Techniques

How many phone calls do you receive each day that involve potential customers enquiring about price? Do you tell them the price immediately? Do they then say "Thank you very much, I'll get back to you" and hang up?

Many clothing stores receive these calls, and many potential clients take the information away and never come back. Good business sense should tell you not to let them get away! When the client makes contact with you, make the most of it.

In this chapter you will find hints, tips and tricks on how to sell more using the telephone including:

How to handle the "How much" question;

Sell to the customer while they are on hold

Use your answering machine/voicemail to generate business

Start selling more and talking less on the telephone now!

#120 REMEMBER MY NAME
As soon as you answer the phone, jot down the caller's name and use it throughout the conversation. People are impressed when you consider their name to be important. But do not overuse it.

#121 GIVE ME INFORMATION
Train your staff never to let a phone call slip through their fingers. Customers don't phone in just to pass the time. They phone for a reason.

The reason is they want someone to provide a service or a product. And if it is not your shop that provides that service, another one will. Let the customer know that you provide more than product alone-you also offer service.

Tell them you have in- house style consultants (you and your staff) and a full range of accessories.

Tell them you have all the high-fashion labels, the latest shipment from overseas, that you are constantly receiving new stock, or that you have contacts in Paris.

Tell them anything about your store but make sure you tell them something.

#122 HOW MUCH IS THAT DRESS

If a customer asks about price, ignore the question as long as you can. Once the customer has heard the answer to their initial question, they will not be so interested in whatever subsequent information you have to offer. You can explain, encourage and build up the stock and your service to your heart's content, but the customer's mind will be centered on the price.

You need to open the lines of communication and build a rapport with the caller to impart this information. So chat with them. Take the emphasis away from giving out information. Redirect your thought processes to converting enquiries into sales, just like a salesman. You are aiming to build the value of the service first. Let the customer know exactly what they will be receiving.

#123 HAVE WE MET?

Ask the client whether they have attended your shop before. This is another way to chat with the caller, to establish rapport and to make a sale all at the same time. Why do you need to know whether they are a regular client? Because if they are not already, your task is to make them one! Choose from some ideas below:

If they have not attended before, tell them it is your policy to offer a discount to new customers.

Tell them all new customers will receive a discount during the current month.

After you do tell the potential customer the price of the service, do not pause. Move the conversation away from the price and towards action, giving the caller less time to feel uncomfortable, compare, analyze and back out.

In short, look at every telephone enquiry as a potential customer. Do not give a simple one-sentence response to a question. Let them see how friendly, cooperative and caring you are. Let them feel that they can trust you, that they will get value for money and quality service. Chances are they will not be able to resist.

#124 HOLD THE LINE PLEASE

Everyone has seen sitcoms or television commercials where the owners of the newly opened business are patiently waiting for customers to arrive. The phone finally rings. They rush to answer it, bowling each other over in the process. Do not do it.

Let the phone ring-for a short while (but no more than five rings). It looks as if you are busy. And if you are busy, the potential customer will think that lots of people must be buying from you. If the business is popular, you must be good. But never let the phone ring out.

Try putting your potential client on hold for a moment. Why? To show the customer your store must be busy. But do not leave them too long, or you will try your customer's patience. They will become frustrated, hang up and go elsewhere. It is a delicate balance.

#125 ADS ON HOLD

A message can be played on the tape while customers are on hold, too. Use the time to advertise your upcoming promotions, your fabulous service and dedication to customers.

Give tips on the latest fashion or any community awards you might have won. Talk about sales or new stock arriving.

Hearing the voice of the owner builds a connection with the client, laying the foundations for future buying.

#126 24 HOUR EMPLOYEE

Use your answering machine to help you. It is an in-house, low-cost, 24-hour-a -day communication tool. Record a message similar to the one you have for putting customers on hold. Keep it short and allow them to leave a message for you if necessary. But change the message according to the current promotion you are running, or to mention any others that you have coming up.

When recording a message for an answering machine, ensure that the greeting is short but very professional. Write it down and practice it several times before recording.

CHAPTER SUMMARY

Now that you finished this chapter you should have an understanding of the following:

How to handle the "How much" question.

Sell to the customer while they are on hold.

Use your answering machine/voicemail to generate business.

End of chapter seven (7).

8 TIME IS MONEY
Strategies for television and radio advertising

Television advertising, done well, is a highly effective way to market your florist shop. It enables you to reach your audience direct; it positions your business as an entity in your community; and it gives you prestige.

The visual element is your best advertising tool. Research shows that most people remember pictures and faces more easily than they remember names, words or slogans.

But television advertising can be expensive. Choosing to run your commercial just once in prime time can blow your whole budget.

In this chapter you will find hints, tips strategies and advice on advertising on television and radio.

Start making sound waves now!

#127 REPEAT REPEAT REPEAT
Advertising of any kind needs to be repeated. It is not enough to run an ad once or twice. It should be constant. The same applies to both radio and television advertising. It is not enough to play your commercial once and then expect people to remember it.

#128 TURN IT UP!
Radio is a fabulous medium for advertising your retail clothing store.

By its nature it is intimate: few people listen to the radio together these days. It is usually listened to while the consumer is alone, at home or in the car. People will even admit they habitually turn the radio on 'for company'. So use it. It is effective. But it is not simply a matter of contacting the radio station and asking to place an ad. There are a number of points you should be aware of to achieve the results you want, before you give your advertising dollars away.

If you are in a region that has more than one radio station to choose from, be aware that some could be described as 'background' stations and others 'foreground'. A background radio station is the style of station that is non-intrusive. It's the kind you can play in the background of a retail store or at home to take the edge off the silence and to give atmosphere. You can still work, think and converse. The foreground station, as you've probably guessed, is more intrusive. It is one that commands listening. Analyze the stations in your area according to this criterion before you approach them.

Think about your target market. Find out what radio stations your customers listen to. Would it be better to place your ad with a rock-and-roll station? A talkback show? Ethnic stations? The news? You could conduct your own little marketing survey and ask your customers what station they listen to, which might help you before you start talking to sales executives.

#129 WHO LISTENS TO THE RADIO

Ask the advertising sales executive of the station for information on their demographics. They will give you written information on the age groups of their listeners, their income, and their place of residence. These things are all important when choosing where to advertise. Otherwise the outcome can be likened to reading Tolstoy to preschool children: the product might be good but the message doesn't get through-making it a waste of your money.

#130 NOT YOUR ONE AND ONLY

You are not restricted to advertising on only one radio station. Choose as many as you like. You can produce your ad independently and distribute it to the stations you choose, which is a cost-effective way of doing it. This works if the stations you select have a similar style and similar target market. It will also work if your business has only one target market.

If your business is diverse and caters to more than one market, consider producing different commercials to place on different radio stations or in different segments to maximize the impact and gain real success for your efforts.

If your style of business is contemporary or creative, choose a more avant-garde station, or select a segment that deals with the arts. If you cater to the young set, choose the popular rock/pop station or time slot. If your market is suburban mums, place your commercial with a more middle- of-the-road station. If you have positioned yourself in the corporate or high-end market, choose drive time on a station that caters to this market.

#131 BEWARE

Beware of the salesman who offers inexpensive rates for radio spots.

Question the choice of station. Question the time slot. Placing a commercial in a time slot that is not going to reach your target market is like reading James Joyce to a sleeping academic: it won't get through, either. So ask the radio station about their 'CUMES'. (The origin of the term is the word 'accumulated'-it refers to their ratings formula.) 'CUMES' relates to the number of listeners that have accumulated every quarter of an hour in the same session.

#132 JINGLE JANGLE

Have you ever had a favorite tune that goes round and round in your head, no matter how hard you try to forget it?

Did you learn your history, multiplication tables or periodic tables by making up a rhyme and adding it to music so you'd remember it for an exam? Did this work, even though you didn't necessarily understand what you were remembering? This is the value of the jingle.

Just about all of us can sing along to the words of songs we last heard years ago, as soon as we hear the familiar melody. The same applies to advertising jingles. We still know the words and the tune of an advertising campaign for a product that was probably removed from the shelves long ago. The jingle stamps a commercial into our long-term memory, seemingly forever.

Jingles attract attention. Do you find yourself turning up the radio when you hear a catchy tune? Do you feel your attention shift and focus on the radio when that tune does come on, rather than remaining involved in your own thoughts?

Jingles aid memory retention. The tune and, with it, the words will attach itself to the mind of the consumer. Every time those words or that tune is heard, the product or service is instantly bought to mind.

Music creates a positive mood. When people are in a positive mood, they are more open to the advertising message. And the positive emotions that become associated with the product or service will be an invaluable selling aid.

#133. HOW DO I GET ONE?

How do you get a jingle? Here are some options, in descending order from the most expensive.

Approach an advertising agency. Agencies will have contacts in the music world. Because it is in their interests to hire the best musical producers, they can usually be relied on to align you with someone good.

You might find this costs you a little more, as you are involving a middleman, but it could be worth it. Don't avoid the new or smaller agencies. They will need to carve their niche in the market and often charge less because of it. And they are probably more used to dealing with smaller budgets.

Approach a musical producer. If you are convinced the person has the equipment, talents and skill, you can go direct to the writer/producer yourself. If you're not so sure, stay with the advertising agency. Again, if there is a newly established producer around, check them out. They are most likely waiting for their lucky break and need to build up their portfolio.

Approach the radio station. The station can create and produce the jingle in-house, and it will probably cost you less. But the effect might not be what you want. It might not stand out from the crowd as you'd hoped, for many reasons. Sometimes it is the writer. Often it is because the same artists and singers are used again and again, making the music sound like all the others. And sometimes they go a bit stale, not keeping abreast of trends.

Search the web. There are many services available to write and produce a jingle for your business. They start from $5 on www.fiverr.com

#123 CREATE A FEELING

A jingle doesn't have to sound down- market. It can be just as classy and innovative as your boutique. Choose the style of music to suit your target market. Use something classical or jazz-like for bridging the gap to a conservative, refined market. Select something more up-tempo or contemporary if you choose to target the youth market. Just define your market and cater to it. The music will draw them in after that.

It is essential to define your market, because by choosing the wrong style of music you will also alienate some sectors. But this can work in your favor by lending a sense of exclusivity. Not many young, headstrong, image-conscious young girls would want to be caught in an 'old ladies' shop'.

Use the jingle to create any feeling you choose; align it with the style you want to project and it will act like bait on a hook to your customers. Image is everything in the fashion industry. It is the reason your customers visit you-so you can improve their image. They will be looking to see whether you project an image that suits them, whether your clothing store looks the way they think it should. The jingle will tell your potential customers what your image is, even before they walk through your door.

#135 MAKE THE MOST OF IT

Once your jingle is produced, make the most of it. Use it at every opportunity for at least two years. The more often you use it, the better. Play it on your telephone on hold and behind the message on your answering machine. Play it in your store. Play it on your television ad, if you advertise on TV. Play it on your radio ad.

Use the top-and-tail, or 'donut', format. Play the tune to catch the attention of the audience at the beginning of the ad, insert in the middle timely information such as new stock or labels, opening hours etc., and finish off with the jingle again.

#136 I SAW IT ON TV

Television advertising, done well, is a highly effective way to market your retail clothing store. It enables you to reach your audience direct; it promotes your business as an entity in your community; it gives you prestige.

Television is a visual medium and the visual element is probably the best advertising weapon. Research shows that people's memories improve 68% if there is a visual they can remember. And customers with a particular product or service 'need' will stamp the image in their minds. Television allows you to show to a broad audience what you have to offer. It allows your clothes to be shown in use, almost as a demonstration. It shows the clothes in context, emphasizing how they can be part of the viewer's lifestyle --or even create it. Both these angles are highly effective selling techniques.

#137 TIME IS MONEY

The timeslot in which you choose to air your commercial can be the most expensive element of television advertising, and therefore potentially the most cost-prohibitive.

A way to repeat your commercial, and not blow your budget, is to choose less expensive spots. Check with your local station to find out when their cheaper times are.

You also need to consider the actual television show in which you select to air your commercial. Not only will it affect the cost of your advertising program but it must be both a show and a time slot that is targeted at your audience. The advertising salesperson will be able to help you. Television stations know who watches what, when.

The less expensive times are during the day and the viewers are predominantly women. You will be able to capture a high portion of your market at this time. A large audience of women could work in your favor. And this equals daytime TV. Because the size of the audience is reduced, the rates will be lower. But because your product is directed at women anyway, the smaller audience size won't compromise your marketing.

#138 THE PLACE WHERE YOU LIVE

The cost of television advertising will depend on the area in which you choose to advertise. It is much less expensive to buy air time on rural television stations than with city broadcasters. The more potential viewers in a time slot or region, the more you can expect to pay to reach them.

While television advertising can be expensive, if you use it to capture the exact market you aim for it can be worth it. And if you choose your times wisely you can build your business to a point that television spots in prime time viewing might well become a business reality.

CHAPTER SUMMARY

Now that you have finished reading this chapter, you should have an understanding of the following:

Whether to run your ad once or more

Whether to advertise in prime time

Different locations affect pricing.

End of chapter eight (8)

9 SOCIAL MONEY
Use social media platforms to grow your business

Social media is an effective way to connect with customers.

There almost as many social media sites as there are clothing designers with new ones popping up every day! To discuss a social media strategy for each of them would make for a very long book. So this chapter will focus on four (4) tried and true social media platforms.

In this chapter you will find hints, tips strategies and advice to grow your business using the following social media platforms:

- Facebook,
- Twitter,
- Instagram,
- Pinterest

Get social now!

#139 KEEP IT SOCIAL

The most important thing to remember when marketing with social media is the word **social**.

People are not using these platforms to be inundated with advertising or getting messages from hundreds of businesses. Do not use the hard sell. Use good, interesting content and do not pressure people.

#140 FACEBOOK ME

Love it or hate it, Facebook is currently the world's biggest social network. It can raise awareness of your store and get people excited about clothes and accessories.

Follow these tips for Facebook success:

- Have a great profile photo, it will set the tone for your page. You could use a photo of your store front, or something from you latest shipment of stock.

- Use the cover photo to showcase more of your stock, or to showcase your shop.
- Post photos of your stock frequently. Take photos of outfits with accessories you stock. Include items from all price brackets, so that all your fans and followers feel like they can afford to buy from your store.
- Post information. For example, post how to mix and match items, post how to accessorize; post the latest trends from overseas.; a what to wear where guide.

The more information you can give away online, the more people will look forward to your posts.

- Promote your auction and shopping nights and any other community events you may have participated in. Remember to post photos of the event after it has occurred.
- Post photos of raffle prize winners in their outfits.

Monthly contests

Running a contest on your Facebook page is a great way to attract followers to your site. Here are some ideas:

- Host a monthly contest for fans of your Facebook page. For example, ask your followers who their favorite style icon is and why. Think up any reason you can.
- Mother's Day contest for people to submit 250 words about how great their mother is, Teachers day, Administrative professional day, and any other day you care to promote. The prize can be a gift voucher from your store.
-

#141 TWITTER

Twitter, the world's second largest social network allows users to post 140-character updates ("tweets") which are shared with their followers.

- Post news, share links, answer questions
- Post information about fashion and current trends, very similar to what you would post on Facebook.
- Promote your monthly contest
- Use custom and popular tags to establish brand values
- Tweet about your auction nights, shopping nights and any community events in which your store is participating.
- Be active in following and retweeting others
- Re-tweet tweets from designers you stock.

#142 INSTAGRAM

Instagram is a visual medium so use it to visually promote your business with great photos of any of the following.

- Photos of your clothing and accessories from all your price brackets. Remember you want your followers to think they can afford to shop in your store.
- Photos of any events your customers may have attended wearing items from your boutique (i.e. weddings, corporate events) - with the customer's permission of course!)
- Photos of contestant winners wearing their prize (with their permission of course).
- Photos of any accessories you stock.

#143 PINTEREST

Pinterest allows users to pin websites, recipes, photos, and maps to virtual pinboards. These boards can be accessed by other users via a feed or search, or boards can be kept private.

Use Pinterest the same way you would use Instagram; promote your business with great photos.

#144 SOCIAL MANAGEMENT

Social media can be a cheap, easy and effective way to promote and grow your retail business. But who has time to post on four or more social platforms every single day!

There are a number of social media management software packages available. Most will let you schedule posts to all of your social media platforms at once.

How do you find them? Simply conduct a google search for Social media management software.

CHAPTER SUMMARY

This chapter contained hints, tips strategies and advice to grow your business using the following social media platforms:

- Facebook,
- Twitter,
- Instagram,
- Pinterest

End chapter nine (9).

THRIVE

Survive and thrive for years to come.

10 RIGHT ON THE MONEY
Keys to long term success

Wow! You have followed all the advice laid out in this book and hopefully have a thriving business.

In this final chapter, you will learn some strategies to keep your business thriving for many years to come.

When you have finished this chapter, you should have an understanding of the following concepts to manage your business.

- Make a statement
- The importance of planning
- The importance of the budget
- The calendar of events

Start planning to stay a little bit longer now!

#145 PERSONAL BEST
Create a personal best program detailing the actions you will take every day to generate new business.

#146 MAKE A STATEMENT
A mission statement can give your business focus and help to clarify, and thus reach goals.

A mission statement is a one-sentence statement that encapsulates the philosophy of your store For example, "French Fashions aims to . . ."etc.

If you are a small retail store not a big organization, do you really need one? The answer is yes.

A mission statement gives your business direction and cohesion. When decisions need to be made and the choice of which way to go is not clear, it will help to return to your mission statement.

Determine the niche that your clothing business will fill. For example:
- Who is your target market?
- What are their needs?
- What is your goal?
- What are your strengths and weaknesses?
- Who is your chief competitor?
- What are their strengths and weaknesses?
- What is your competitor's target market?

To develop your own mission statement and to make things clear, complete the following:

The purpose of (insert your business name) is to.......
The target market will be....
The purpose will be achieved by positioning the service in the following way....
Marketing tools to be used will be...
Cost of marketing will be $....

When you have completed your mission statement, use it like a roadmap to see where you are going. When you can see where you are going you can monitor your progress towards your destination.

#147 HERE TODAY, GONE TOMORROW

Every business and marketing guru will tell you that you must spend money advertising and marketing your business.

"But I'm a small clothing store, why should I?" you ask "I haven't really got the money to spend. Besides, how do you know it works? And anyway, I advertise now and then, when I think of it. Or when I can afford it. Won't that do?" In a word: no. Here are some reasons why:
- The market is constantly changing.
- People forget
- People will spend where they are told
- Strengthen your position
- Make new customers; and
- Keep your old customers

The market is constantly changing. Think about the families who move out of town. What about those who move into town? Think of the youngsters who will grow into adults, get married, and have babies. You need to constantly market your business because the world is not static.

People forget. Sad but true. Research indicates that only 63% of readers remembered brand names and specific advertising after a 13-week campaign. One month after that same campaign, only 32% of respondents could recall the brand advertising message. You must keep telling them who you are, where you are, and what you offer.

People will spend where they are told. Customers need to buy. You have to tell them you have what they want. How else will they know? If customers are not reminded of your business, they will spend their money with another clothing store.

Strengthen your position. People are attracted to strength. Customers like stability. Look solid, established, known. They like stability. Your clothing stop will attract people if it has been around for a period of time and enjoys a good reputation, built up over years of marketing. If it is new, the marketing approach you employ can give it a feeling of good, solid backing.

Make new customers. You cannot start a business without marketing. It shows that you exist.

Keep your old customers. It costs five to seven times more to get new customers than it costs to retain them. But even your regulars will become bored with your routine, be poached by someone else or just plain forget about you-unless you refresh their memories.

#148 CALENDAR OF EVENTS

A marketing calendar is an essential tool for maximizing your profit. Without it your boutique will drift along, week by week, hoping to make money. Without your calendar you are underutilizing your opportunity for making more profit.

Think of the different types of marketing strategies available to you. Choose the ones that are compatible, that you are able to employ and to use regularly.

Make a promotions calendar using the following steps:

a. Work out when your quiet times of the year are, and plan promotions for those spots.
b. Work out how many promotions you will need for the year.
c. Work on promotion concepts for the quiet times.
d. Look at your past successful promotions and repeat them. Also look at other companies' successful campaigns. What made them stand out? Can you replicate it?
e. Look at your past not-so-successful promotions and see what you can learn.
f. Stagger your marketing techniques. Avoid using blocks of advertising in only one medium.
g. Change the lengths of your campaigns, to achieve a healthy balance.

But remember to allow periods during which there are no special sales, to give credibility to the sales that you do have.

#149 THE IMPORTANCE OF ADVERTISING AND MARKETING BUDGET

As a business owner it is important for you to track where your dollars are going, especially your advertising and marketing dollars.

Keeping track of the expenditure shows how effective your advertising actually is, and helps you quantify advertising dollars with a rate of redemption (in simple speak, the percentage of sales you achieve per advertising dollar spent).

Money spent on marketing is a reinvestment in your business, so the closer to 5% of sales you can spend, the better. Of course, your other financial commitments will also affect whether you can allow for 5%.

For example, if your projected gross sales for the year were $200,000 your advertising budget would be $10,000.

This money is usually allocated to the traditional forms of media. You can also have a miscellaneous budget, to support non-traditional or creative forms of marketing to be implemented in a spur-of-the-moment style.

Break down your budget by media, focusing on those which are best suited to your geographic region (city or country) and the demographics (age, sex and income) of your target market. As an example of how to do this:

- *Direct mail*: flyers 10c apiece x 10 000 = $1000
- *Radio*: slots during drive time 100 X $50 = $5000
- *Television*: one short regional ad campaign = $2000
- *Miscellaneous*: promotional material not planned = $2000

(Note: The television budget will depend solely on the area you live in. This example has been based on a short campaign run in a regional area. City-based rates will differ from regional rates.)

The budgeting process allows you stick to a certain expenditure, and limits sporadic spending. All too often small businesses will under advertise until business starts to fall off, then overcompensate with a rushed campaign of panic advertising that costs too much.

The budget allows you to use a variety of media to target your market, also to measure the success of the advertising you undertake. It need not be a technical financial breakdown but rather a general spending plan for your advertising dollars. Do not start the year without one!

#150 SLIM DOWN TO BOOST YOUR BOTTOM LINE

Increase your profits by reducing your expenses. 'No problem. Common business procedure: you say. But how? Hold out for the last-minute rush

Know the deadlines for ads in the local newspapers, radio and regional television. Often you can get a cheaper rate for ad space by waiting until the last minute to take advantage of unsold space (but be warned, you may miss out altogether). Check out the deadlines of magazines specific to your specialty. For instance, in many city areas there are sections in newspapers or magazines aimed directly at the fashion/ retail industry. Some you will find on street corners, others in newsagents.

#151 BUDGET BUDGET BUDGET

Save money and save your business-stick to a budget! The most common causes of failure in budgeting are: unrealistic goals; quitting too soon; and misunderstanding what a budget really is (i.e. a way of ensuring that your incomings are greater than your outgoings).

CHAPTER SUMMARY

Now that you have finished this chapter, you should have an understanding of the following concepts to manage your business.

- Make a statement
- The importance of planning
- The importance of the budget
- The calendar of events

THE BUCK STOPS HERE
The final tip

#152 HAVE FUN!

Whatever you choose to focus on when marketing your clothing store, remember it will all work better if you enjoy it. So take a light hearted approach and experiment with a range of promotions to get your name and image firmly established in the public eye.

Learn from everyone you can, whether it is national chains or local stores. Learn from business ides that work. Learn from business ideas that do not work. If it works, do more of it. If it does not work, learn from it. And remember your small florist can be a lot more flexible and responsive than a huge hierarchical corporation. So make this your small business advantage. Enjoy.

Good luck with your business and thank you for reading this book.

ABOUT THE AUTHOR

Brendan Power is the author of The Small Business Success Guide; a series of books on small business marketing and operations.

The Small Business Success Guides are written by Brendan with the input of small business owners.

A small business owner himself, Brendan was born in a pub. He grew up working in his father's hotels, then later in his father's brewery. In addition, Brendan has owned and operated a number of pubs in Australia and the United States of America.

Brendan also has extensive background in marketing. He has worked in the United States of America for an American based brewer and was Managing Director of a company that specialized in the management of hotels, restaurants and cafes. He was also the CEO of an international backpacking company.

He currently spends his time writing, consulting to small business owners and helping his wife with the school run.

Brendan has Bachelor of Business and an MBA and a graduate of the Australian Institute of Company Directors.

Printed in Great Britain
by Amazon